LETS GO

PUBLISH!

Millennials Say America Was 'Never That Great'

Many are pleased that the days of Americans as political chumps are not over!

Learn what Millennials think of America by reading this book. It is the best thing you can do to understand why our second youngest generation is ambivalent about our great country and its founding. This book not only gives the millennial perspective, it is the best starter book for anybody wanting to refresh their knowledge or learn about America, its founding and how its basic principles of government assure our freedom and liberty. Freedom and liberty may not be too important for many millennials but for most Americans, there is nothing more important.

America's founders were smart, intelligent, and selfless men. When Pennsylvania's Benjamin Franklin said: "We must indeed all hang together or most assuredly, we shall all hang separately, he gave away the essence of the seriousness of the task facing America's founders. For as trite as some seem to portray the founding today, it was a serious undertaking by serious men who had been pushed around enough by King George. There is no reason from anybody to be ashamed of America today or its founding.

Though millennials may take issue with the founding, few are packing up and heading to greener pastures. The world looks at America oppositely from the view of millennials that America was 'never that great." Millions of non-Americans come to our shores legally and illegally every year because they want to enjoy the American Dream, which still exists only in America.

When asked why so many seek to come to America, a typical answer is like this: "Compared to a lot of countries,… people have the opportunity to have more freedom… their kids to have a better education… in general, a better life compared to what they would have if they stayed in their home country… can't blame them… if I lived in a 3rd world country, I would be packing my bags too."

Another reason cited is that the government takes care of the people in the US to a fault. "…this is the only country where a person can sit on his butt all day and have his needs met by the welfare system… in most 3rd world countries, a person cannot meet his needs even by slaving all day." The world comes to America willingly because America is great and has been great and life is better in the US than anyplace else.

It is unfortunate, however, that our country is led by corrupt and greedy politicians who have taken control of many levels of governments in America. The good news is that most US citizens and others are hopping on the Train of Freedom to win back America from the forces of evil. Millennials are slow to learn but over time, they too will get the real message.

This book is today's solution for *would-be* chumps to be better prepared to react to the overreach of praetorian politicians and elite establishmentarians, who hope to set the country back three hundred years. With statements like 'America was never great,' it shows they would be happy to replace freedom with a hand-out-based government that controls the people and not vice-versa. Freedom loving people from across the world come here for freedom and opportunity. Those in this country who may say that America is not a great country should take a one-way trip to Russia or Mexico. Good riddance! Too bad they won't.

This book is a quick way for you to learn about the real America and not the misimpressions of millennials and socialist progressive whackos. This book shows why the many blessings of our founding principles need not be replaced.

Just because corrupt and powerful officials choose to ignore the rights and freedoms of American citizens does not mean we must endure their tyranny. The first step of course is to understand the founding and the most basic written precepts describing America and our rights as Americans. Reading this book about America's greatness is a must for every US citizen. I bet you will not be able to put this book down.

BRIAN W. KELLY

Title   **Millennials Say America Was 'Never That Great'**
Copyright © 2014,2018   Brian W. Kelly
Editor: Brian P. Kelly
Author: Brian W. Kelly

Disclaimer: Though judicious care was taken throughout the writing and the publication of this work that the information contained herein is accurate, there is no expressed or implied warranty that all information in this book is 100% correct. Therefore, neither LETS GO PUBLISH, nor the author accepts liability for any use of this work.

Trademarks: A number of products and names referenced in this book are trade names and trademarks of their respective companies.

Referenced Material: *Standard Disclaimer: The information in this book has been obtained through personal and third-party observations, interviews, and copious research. Where unique information has been provided or extracted from other sources, those sources are acknowledged within the text of the book itself or at the end of the chapter in the Sources Section. Thus, there are no formal footnotes nor is there a bibliography section. Any picture that does not have a source was taken from various sites on the Internet with no credit attached. If resource owners would like credit in the next printing, please email publisher.*

```
Published by:    LETS GO PUBLISH!
Editor           Brian P. Kelly
Editor           Brian P. Kelly
Cover Design     Brian W Kelly
Web site         www.letsgopublish.com
Library of Congress Copyright Information Pending
```
Book Cover Design by Brian W. Kelly

ISBN Information: The International Standard Book Number (ISBN) is a unique machine-readable identification number, which marks any book unmistakably. The ISBN is the clear standard in the book industry. 159 countries and territories are officially ISBN members. The Official ISBN for this book is also on the outside cover: _____

978-1-947402-57-7

The price for this work is: **$9.95 USD**
10   9   8   7   6   5   4   3   2   1

Release Date: September 2018

Dedication

To my two best friends,

Dennis Grimes and Gerry Rodski.

Thank you for all of your support in my writing and publishing efforts.

You guys are the best.

Acknowledgments

In every book that I write or edit, I publicly acknowledged all of the help that I have received from many sources. Some of these wonderful people are still on earth and others have made their way to heaven.

I would like to thank many people for helping me in this effort. I appreciate all the help that I received in putting this book together, along with the 66 other books from the past.

My printed acknowledgments were once so large that book readers needed to navigate too many pages to get to page one of the text. To permit me more flexibility, I put my acknowledgment list online at www.letsgopublish.com. The list of acknowledgments continues to grow. Believe it or not, it once cost about a dollar more to print each book.

Thank you all on the big list in the sky and God bless you all for your help.

Please check out www.letsgopublish.com to read the latest version of my heartfelt acknowledgments updated for this book. Thank you all!

In this book, I received some extra special help from many avid Notre Dame supporters including Bruce Ikeda, Dennis Grimes, Gerry Rodski, Angel Brent Evans, Wily Ky Eyely, Angel Irene McKeown Kelly, Angel Edward Joseph Kelly Sr., Angel Edward Joseph Kelly Jr., Ann Flannery, Angel James Flannery Sr., Mary Daniels, Bill Daniels, Robert Gary Daniels, Angel Sarah Janice Daniels, Angel Punkie Daniels, Joe Kelly, Diane Kelly, Brian P. Kelly, Mike P. Kelly, Katie P. Kelly, Angel Ben Kelly, and Budmund (Buddy) Arthur Kelly.

Preface

Here we are citizens in a truly exceptional country. Yet, even here in America all is not perfect. And so, if we the people do not smarten up, things will get a lot worse and they may never get better again. Only in America would a group of young people dubbed as millennials enjoy the very freedoms which they complain about

Our country and our government and many people including leftist socialist progressives such as Andrew Cuomo and too many millennials to count are out of touch with America's founding. They don't understand the richness of this country brought to us all by the founders but they think they know it all.

America has its share of issues for sure but we are still free to change it. According to the founders, it was not supposed to be this way. Taxes are too high, elected officials are out of touch, government is too big, spending is out of control; the new healthcare program is a train wreck, the federal government is incompetent, the people too little a voice in government, too many people are too lazy to hold government accountable. Besides all that, too many of the nation's supposed best people are on the take… There's lots more!

Learn what Millennials and other whiners and complainers think of America by reading this book. It is the best thing you can do to understand why our second youngest generation is ambivalent about our great country and its founding. This book not only gives the millennial perspective, it is the best starter book for anybody wanting to refresh their knowledge or learn about the real America for the first time.

In this book you will learn about our great country; why it is great; its risky and dangerous founding and how its basic principles of government assure our freedom and liberty. Freedom and liberty may not be too important for many millennials but for most Americans, there is nothing more important other than life itself.

You will learn that America's founders were smart, intelligent, and selfless men. When Pennsylvania's Benjamin Franklin said: "We must indeed all hang together or most assuredly, we shall all hang separately," he gave away the essence of the seriousness of the task facing America's founders. For as trite as some seem to portray the founding today, it was a serious undertaking by serious men who had been pushed around more than enough by King George. There is no reason from anybody to be ashamed of America today or its founding.

Though millennials may take issue with the greatness of the founding, few are packing up and heading to greener pastures. The world looks at America oppositely from the view of millennials that America was 'never that great." Millions of non-Americans come to our shores legally and illegally every year because they want to enjoy the American Dream, which still exists only in America.

When asked why so many seek to come to America, a typical answer is like this: "Compared to a lot of countries,… people have the opportunity to have more freedom… their kids to have a better education… in general, a better life compared to what they would have if they stayed in their home country… can't blame them… if I lived in a 3rd world country, I would be packing my bags too."

Another reason cited is that the government takes care of the people in the US to a fault. "…this is the only country where a person can sit on his butt all day and have his needs met by the welfare system… in most 3rd world countries, a person cannot meet his needs even by slaving all day." The world comes to America willingly because America is great and has been great and life is better in the US than any other option in the entire world.

It is unfortunate, however, that our country is led by corrupt and greedy politicians who have taken control of many levels of governments in America. The good news is that most US citizens and others are hopping on the Train of Freedom to win back America from these forces of evil. Millennials are slow to learn but over time, they too will get the real message.

This book is today's solution for *would-be* chumps to be better prepared to react to the overreach of praetorian politicians and elite establishmentarians, who hope to set the country back three hundred years. With statements like 'America was never great,' it shows they would be happy to replace freedom with a hand-out-based government that controls the people and not vice-versa. Freedom loving people from across the world come here for freedom and opportunity. Those who live in this country who may say that America is not a great country, should take a one-way trip to Russia or Mexico. Good riddance! Too bad they won't.

This book is a quick way for you to learn about the real America and not the misimpressions of millennials and socialist progressive whackos. This book shows why the many blessings of our founding principles need not be replaced.

Just because corrupt and powerful officials choose to ignore the rights and freedoms of American citizens does not mean we must endure their tyranny. The first step of course is to understand the founding and the most basic written precepts describing America and our rights as Americans. Reading this book about America's greatness is a must for every US citizen. I bet you will not be able to put this book down.

Yes, you can learn about America by reading this book. It is the best thing you can do to understand our great country and our great form of government, before the bad guys are empowered to take it away from us.

This book is the best starter book for anybody wanting to refresh their knowledge or learn about the founding of America and the government of the United States of America. This book is a way that all citizens can use to be better prepared to react to the overreach of today's corrupt politicians.

Without the knowledge that you can gain so easily in this book, for example, you might unknowingly sign up for a socialist progressive government that takes away your rights, and makes you dependent on government employees for the rest of your natural life.

Today more than ever, having experienced our prior President and his coterie in their "resistance, trying to usurp the power of our new duly elected president, we citizens are in imminent danger. We cannot let them succeed.

We just went through a period in which the chief executive ignored the Constitution and administered the office of the presidency in a lawless fashion. We can never let this happen again. Americans need to know their rights and protections built into the basic framework of our government. The very worst thing we can do as Americans is give up these protections to a self-serving promise-everything group of elite liberal-progressive socialists. Our freedoms will be gone and will not come back on their own.

Just because one powerful group of people choose to ignore our rights and freedoms does not mean we must endure their tyranny. The first step of course is to understand America's discovery; its revolution, its founding, and its most basic written precepts. I repeat that reading this book is a must for every US citizen.

If you have been paying attention to what is going on in America today, you know that just a few years ago during the past administration, we were in deep trouble. We had a busted economy, high unemployment, no jobs, and our basic rights to freedoms such as speech, religion, the press, and our right-to-bear-arms were being impinged upon.

The founders saw it as a civic duty for Americans to *pay attention* to our government so that we could avoid being chumps and being snookered by crooked politicians. The people of America paid attention and elected a responsible president and a new administration that have already made great inroads to "Making America Great Again!"

You and I know that there are more issues than just those noted above, and we must fix them quickly while we still have an America and while we have a president who is a friend of the people. This was our shame and it will be our shame again if we let the corruption rampant in the country today to being about the fall of a government that is finally of, by, and for the people of America. I think that is why you bought this book. Thank you very much.

We are on the same side, and together we can all help. We first must understand that Millennials are wrong. America has been great from its founding. We had some bad years from 2009 through 2016 and even before that but our dark days, the days in which millennials formed their personalities were during this time period.

Despite the current opinion of too many millennials. About what is going on, we must understand our rights. Even before you and me and everybody else are on board, you must start the first wave of solutions by opening your windows all the way and shouting as loud as we can: "I am mad as hell, and I am not going to take it anymore." Now, didn't that feel better? That may be all it takes if you are a bit concerned about your country.

Then, after you read this book, you must make sure that you talk to other citizens out there—those that you know—people like you and I and others, and let's help them know that it is time. It is time to get off the couch and act. Unless we all fully engage in America, when we wake up from our deep fog, there may be no America left for our progeny. We will have blown it for sure if we permit that to happen.

In this book, we unabashedly recommend that you stop trusting government, whether run by Republicans or Democrats, since it is clearly not working for our best interests. The sooner we can understand the active threat from the left and the passive threat from the right, the sooner we can move on to solving the problem for our values, our country, and our freedom. There is even room for millennials to see the light.

It will be tough to wage this war against the corrupt politicians and the corrupt media if we are not even permitted to help on the battlefield when America is hanging by just a thread. The smarter we are, the more chances we have for success.

There is no question that a number of Americans—Democrat and Republican have had enough. That is why Donald Trump is our new President. Trump representing everything that Americans view as a solution to the ills of government as practiced for too many years— especially the eight years of our former anti-American president. President Trump is different thank God, and that difference gave him a big edge, and that edge is helping him save our great country.

President Trump pledged to "drain the swamp" of DC corruption, and he promised to renegotiate NAFTA, build a wall to favor Americans over illegal aliens, and he promised to repeal and replace Obamacare and rid the country of a burdensome tax system. Much of that has happened and if we give him a Congress full of good Americans and not leftist Democrats, he will get it all done for us.

Unfortunately, as you know, there are a group of people in his own political party and half of the Congress– the Democrats (Pelosi, Schumer, Watters, and company) who have decided to not give the people the government we elected. And, so it is our duty to take what is not being given to President Trump. In this book, we explain how we got here and what we can do about it from here on in to assure our greatness.

Your author, Brian W. Kelly has been writing books to help Americans for years. He monitors what is happening to our government and he has written extensively in book form and in hundreds of articles about the major problems our country faces.

Kelly is one of America's most outspoken and eloquent conservative spokesmen. He is the author of No Amnesty! No Way!, *Saving America, Taxation Without Representation*, , Kill the EPA!, *Jobs! Jobs! Jobs!*, *The Federalist Papers*, etc.—a total of 173 books. All books are available at amazon.com/author/brianwkelly in both paperback (Amazon) and eBook (Kindle) form.

Like many Americans, Brian is fed up with a stifling socialist progressive Marxists sitting in too many top seats in Washington, DC. The progressives place the needs of everybody else in front of the needs of Americans. Like many Americans, Kelly is shocked and in some ways frightened at how brazen our former President had become in ignoring our Constitution.

Brian Kelly has read the founding documents, the underlying intelligence reports, and he has researched and written about such topics for years. As noted, Brian has written one hundred seventy-three books and hundreds of articles before penning this book about our Great America. He is deeply concerned about how intolerable the results of poor government policy can be within our neighborhoods and our lives. After walking us through history and showing the problems in government today, Kelly's comprehensible and sane recommendations in this book are explained in detail within the covers of this soon-to-be classic edition.

More and more Americans are clamoring for jobs but all that has been given by the government to the people is lip service. Both parties permit it. Americans want to keep their health insurance and pick their own doctors, and they want to be able to afford the insurance. We are sick of lies and the insinuation of Russia Collusion as an excuse to give Democrats a victory when they scored a record loss. If our past president had put his name to a plan like the plan Trump is using to restore America, he too might have won our support. Instead, he lied to the people and everything in healthcare is worse than in 2009 and the country was falling apart when Trump began the process of rebuilding America.

The Presidency is not the only area of national government that has been in trouble. Americans who know their rights voted out the party of the past president and must be ready to vote out scoundrels from the Congress and the Senate to protect America and Americans. A Congress that does not support the people's president must be voted out of office.

In his eight years, the prior president tried to take away our guns; ram a health scam on Americans that includes death panels for the elderly and infirm; grant illegals citizenship while handing them benefits paid by hard working Americans, including free education; and finally, he encouraged foreigners to take more American jobs. His party was punished by Americans in 2016 with the election of a president from the Republican Party, a newcomer, a nationalist and populist conservative, Donald J. Trump.

The title of this book, *Millennials say America Was "Never That Great,"* is a title to get your attention for sure. But it is more than that. It is a real problem that we now face in America as a generation of Americans with great potential have been led astray by coffee-breath professors in Academia.

Brian W. Kelly knows that corrupt academicians and politicians want to make suckers and chumps out of all Americans, so they can advance their personal and group-think agendas. Kelly does not want Americans to trust the politicians from the Swamp. Like W. C. Fields, politicians are not about to give a sucker an even break or smarten up a chump. After the chapters in this book, you will no longer be content with being a sucker or a chump and you will work hard to win back America for the sake of your freedom and liberty and that of your progeny.

You are going to love this book since it is designed by an American for Americans. Few books are a must-read but Millennials say America Was "Never That Great," will quickly appear at the top of America's most read list. If we do not gain back the greatness of our America somebody may take it from us?

Sincerely,

Brian P. Kelly, Editor

Table of Contents

About the Author

Brian W. Kelly retired as an Assistant Professor in the Business Information Technology (BIT) program at Marywood University, where he also served as the IBM i and midrange systems technical advisor to the IT faculty. Kelly has designed, developed, and taught many college and professional courses. He is also a contributing technical editor to a number of IT industry magazines, including "The Four Hundred" and "Four Hundred Guru" published by IT Jungle.

Kelly is a former IBM Senior Systems Engineer and he has been a candidate for US Congress and the US Senate from Pennsylvania. He has an active information technology consultancy. He is the author of 173 books and hundreds of articles. Kelly is a frequent speaker at COMMON, IBM conferences, and other technical conferences. Ask him to speak at your next conservative / nationalist rally!

Over the past twenty years, Brian Kelly has become America's most outspoken and eloquent conservative protagonist. Besides *Just Say No to Chris Christie for President*, Kelly is also the author of *No Amnesty! No Way!*, *Taxation Without Representation*, and many other patriotic books.

Endorsed by the Independence Hall Tea Party in 2010, Kelly ran for Congress against a 13-term Democrat; he took no campaign contributions, spent enough to buy signs and T-shirts, and as a virtual unknown, he captured 17% of the vote— www.briankellyforcongress.com. Kelly then supported Republican challenger Lou Barletta, a conservative leader on immigration policy, and helped him win a resounding victory in the general election. Barletta is now running for the US Senate in PA. Like you, Brian Kelly loves America and thinks the country is great!.

Chapter 1 Andrew Cuomo and Millennials Re: A "Great" America

Near the end of August 2018, those with beating hearts in America were taken back by the words of New York Governor Andrew Cuomo. The Governor later found himself in some hot water with conservatives and those professing to love America after he claimed that President Trump's "Make America Great Again" slogan is inaccurate.

Cuomo took disrespect for America to a new level with an off the cuff remark when he said that America was never great to start with. Some Americans are asking the soon to be former Governor of the country also bad for his dad, Mario, or is it just Andrew? Was it tough growing up as a well-to-do white person in America? What do you really think Governor Cuomo?

The twice-elected governor of New York State, whose father was also elected governor twice, disrespected everyone who has fought for this country and worked hard every day to create a better life for themselves and their neighbors.

Ever since the United States was founded on the notion of life, liberty and the pursuit of happiness, generations of families have worked day in and day out to build a better life. All occupations, whether it be farmers, bankers, coal miners, firefighters, policemen or salesmen enjoyed unprecedented success in America. There is something great in each and every individual getting up every morning and grinding through the day to improve their lives and the lives of those around them. There is something great in a company that allows all people to be successful, regardless of their backgrounds.

Nobody is asking anybody to worship America blindly without recognizing that our believed country does not have some bumps and bruises on its record. We fought a war to free slaves but we won their freedom. We have grown and evolved, and like anything great in life, we still have room as a country to grow and evolve even more.

America cannot become complacent with where we are, but that doesn't mean we need to look back on our history with distain such as the leftist Governor Cuomo does. He has chosen to completely neglect and disrespect everything good this country has done. With the statement he made, he threw away the sacrifices of millions of people to make this country a beacon of hope, a shining city on a hill, as President Reagan was famous for saying.

More and more Americans believe that we must hold Governor Cuomo accountable for his callous remarks about our country. Hopefully he does not represent the values of all New Yorkers. Come this November, the people of New York cannot forget these nasty comments that he made when he showed his true colors about America.

For all but about ten percent full-leftist activists in America, Cuomo's statement was unwelcome and unexpected. For somebody wanting most of America to love him unconditionally, enough to make him their president, it was an incredible statement. His dissing of America showed bankruptcy was the top "virtue" of Democratic ideals. Cuomo must have been pretty sure of himself to make such a remark but he is 100% wrong. His act was simply a pompous overture to help endear him to the far leftists.

Yes, Governor. Andrew Cuomo did the unthinkable. It may not hurt him as he faces a goofy far-left "Sex and the City" actress Cynthia Nixon in the Democratic Primary for re-election on Sept. 13. Who knows how New Yorkers, who have had enough Cuomo for years will react but as a group, they are leftists.

For some reason, the fact that Dear Andrew is considering a race for the Democratic presidential nomination in 2020, did not cause him to feel constrained as he dissed America. He felt compelled to tell us all that America isn't great, it's never been great and it's not going to be great again. "We're not going to make America great again; it was never that great," Cuomo contemptuously remarked. He certainly was not taught American exceptionalism as he must have attended a very forward thinking liberal school.

As lemmings waiting for their next instructions, millennials as a group have found favor with the Governor's comments. The fake-news media could not be more pleased that somebody is picking on America.

This is not the first time that the media has jumped on a set of ill-advised Cuomo remarks.

There are many who recall that New York's chief executive asked conservatives not to visit NY State as we would not be welcome. The official state motto of NY is Excelsior, which is most often translated as "ever upward." However, in Cuomo's last major gaffe several years ago, it was obvious that if Governor Andrew Cuomo had his way, he'd prefer it to say "ever liberal."

What about conservatives for an *ever liberal* state? Machs Nichts! Cuomo told conservative Republicans– specifically anyone who is pro-traditional marriage, pro-life or pro-guns – they "have no place in the state of New York". How's them apples? Does Cuomo have a shot at the presidency? I don't think so

Some people (maybe the 10% leftists cited above) liked Cuomo's giving America a historical black eye. Millennials of course looked at this as an opportunity to also slam America. I captured a few comments by Cuomo followers about the Governor's thinking on America.

When asked if there was ever a time in America's history when America was great, the majority of the people in the liberal section of NY where the sample was taken made sure the interviewer knew they were siding with Governor Cuomo.

Most conservatives would figure goofy New Yorkers, who will have nothing to do with this book, are part of the sick puppies who helped Hillary Clinton win New York's 29 electoral votes. Clinton had 1,736,590 more votes than Donald J. Trump, with 100 percent reporting. That's how sick New Yorkers can be for their leftist causes. That explains perfectly the disrespect Cuomo has for our country.

A typical response was like this: "I don't believe America has been great for all folks, ever…even today," said one respondent, while another added simply, "I would have to agree with Governor Cuomo." One person elaborated on their reasoning for saying America was never great, saying, "The idea that there was this once great America is pointing towards this false sense of nationalism…What, it's talking about is white America? Yeah, it's not great."

Another respondent cited similar points, declaring that "America has been great…for straight white men."

Anybody paying attention to how coffee-breath professors indoctrinate students such as college age millennials know that the thought process on America has a lot to do with what has been taught in the classroom. Forget about American exceptionalism, the loonie-lefty professors in academia have no such leanings. If you are wondering if anybody said America was great. Of course they did but that is not what the lefty news media would consider prime news material.

Anita M Ayers commented about the strangeness of millennials: "They are products of a school system inundated with far left ideology. If they had been raised with the actual history of the USA they would understand how truly great she is."

"So this is from kids that have been giving everything. Everyone gets a trophy. The one who works and dedicates himself to hard work is not set apart. Show up on graduation day and get a diploma no grades no attendance. Sad." Another said that "every external environment is relative. Its why you have a lot of rich people that have always had money aren't always happy. Being able to accurately gauge bad/avg/good/great/etc., someone needs to have experienced contrast…They haven't. Their most vivid memories are from the Obama years."

"I think we ship them all off to Venezuela… Russia… wherever they think is great." "Show me a better place than America and Ill go there myself. Lets compare the past 200 years in America with Europe and the rest of the world."

"I say get out of our Country then and for you kids… get out of our country if you think our country is not great go to some foreign country and see how long you would last there."

PJMedia offered the following contrast with the Third Reich:

"Hitler once said, "He alone, who owns the youth, gains the future." Totalitarians like Hitler and Lenin knew that any opposition by the population to their policies would be erased in a couple of generations if they could capture the minds of young people".

"Hitler had the Hitler Youth. Lenin, the Young Communist League. In the case of the Hitler Youth, membership was eventually made mandatory. The Young Communist League was seen as a vital stepping stone to the good life for children in the Soviet Union."

"I bring this up because while conservatives were busy making tons of money in the '80s, '90s, and early 2000s, liberals were busy taking over the entire educational establishment. The fruits of their labors? A couple of generations of kids who are clueless about the complete history of the country they grew up in."

When have you met a millennial whose rantings made any sense?

Kyle Becker writing in Lifezette had this to say:

"It's another stunning display of ignorance from today's sheltered millennials.

After New York Gov. Andrew Cuomo caused a stir on Saturday with his comment that America "was never that great," Campus Reform interviewed college students to see if they agreed with the Democratic governor. (Cuomo partially walked back his comments in a weird, PR-issued statement afterward.)

"I don't believe America has been great for all folks, ever. Even today," one person responded to the query. I would have to agree with Gov. Cuomo," that student added.

"The idea that there was this once-great America is pointing toward this false sense of nationalism," another said. "What — it's talking about white America? Yeah, you know, it's not great."

" Several students also said they had never heard any discussion, lectures or classroom instruction whatsoever by their teachers about why this country — their native land, the home of their birth, the place so many dream of living and thriving in — is great."

There is no question that millennials are a special breed of cat and there is no question that America is the greatest place to live on earth.

Chapter 2 Generations—Boomers, Millennials, X,Y, Z, & Others

MULTIPLE GENERATIONS @ WORK

Five Generations Working Side by Side in 2020

TRADITIONALISTS Born 1900-1945	BOOMERS Born 1946-1964	GEN X Born 1965-1976	MILLENNIAL Born 1977-1997	GEN 2020 After 1997
Great Depression	Vietnam, Moon Landing	Fall of Berlin Wall	9/11 Attacks	Age 15 and Younger
World War II	Civil/Women's Rights	Gulf War	Community Service	Optimistic
Disciplined	Experimental	Independent	Immediacy	High Expectations
Workplace Loyalty	Innovators	Free Agents	Confident, Diversity	Apps
Move to the 'Burbs	Hard Working	Internet, MTV, AIDS	Social Everything	Social Games
Vaccines	Personal Computer	Mobile Phone	Google, Facebook	Tablet Devices

Each generation brings its own view of the world, which creates both opportunities and threats to businesses. This demands Generational Intelligence!

MULTIPLE GENERATIONS @ WORK SURVEY

Most people "know" millennials

I recently wrote two books about millennials. Both had catchy titles:

1. Deport All Millennials Now!
2. Millennials Are People Too!

Ironically, when introduced to the two books, most Americans that I interviewed have little problem with deporting millennials if

It were only possible. Moreover, most people were not interested in learning more about the humanity of millennials as they are OK with their unfavorable impressions of this huge block of young Americans. Looking at the cover title, they did not think my book suggesting *millennials are people too* would help them change their opinions. Finding out that millennials disrespect America along with Andrew Cuomo does nothing for this prevailing negative opinion by most Americans .

Since this book that you are reading is primarily about millennials, as well as the goodness and greatness of America and its representative form of government, before we do anything else let's define a millennial? A millennial is part of a specific generation of births.

Generations provide researchers the opportunity to look at Americans both by their place in the life cycle – whether a young adult, a middle-aged parent or a retiree – and by their membership in a cohort of individuals who were born at a similar time.

The Pew Research Center is one of many who study trends in age groups on various issues. They choose to use 1996 as the last birth year for millennials in their analyses. Others go as far as 2002. Thus, anyone born between 1981 and 1996 (ages 22 to 37 in 2018) will be considered a Millennial, and, according to Pew, anyone born from 1997 onward will be part of a new generation.

Since the oldest among this rising generation are just turning 21 this year, and most are still in their teens, the Pew Research Center believes that it is too early to give the "post millennials" a name. But, this does not prevent other groups from naming them.

You will hear terms such as Generation Z or Gen Z (also known as the iGeneration, iGen and Post-Millennials) used to describe the generation after millennials. Most of Generation Z have used the Internet since a young age, and they are generally comfortable with technology and with interacting on social media

Experts suggest that the emphasis on naming generations comes from companies who want to sell something to a specific age group and want a convenient way of referring to a group. We will take a shot at naming all the generations in this chapter.

"Millennial" as a term was coined in the late 1980s by the consultants Neil Howe and William Strauss. Both of these gentlemen are baby boomers and were "boomers" long before the term Generation X was even popularized. (They wanted to call millennials the "13th Gen," but that didn't stick, and neither did "slackers.").

What is a generation?

It is easy to get your mix all talked up in today's crazy world of classifying and labelling generations of human beings based on when they were born. And, so we now have jargon in use today that expects everybody to understand certain phrases such as "Gen X," "Baby Boomer", "The Greatest Generation," etc.

To be able to engage in regular conversation with most people today, it helps Americans to have a reasonably good idea of what these and other generational terms actually mean. Without necessarily knowing a particular generation, most of us at least have an idea as to what comprises a generation. In my day, we used the term generation to refer to a 20-year period in duration, but it means a bit more than that today.

It would be more correct today to say that a generation is a group of people *born* around the same time and *raised* around the same place. People in a particular "birth cohort," or generation, often exhibit similar characteristics, preferences, and values over their lifetimes

If somebody says to you, for example, "Oh, that happened three generations ago," how long ago might that be. Fifty years ago, the answer would simply be 20 years times 3 generations equals 60 years. Not today.

We still reckon the passage of time by generations, especially for those indefinite periods measured by a number of successive parent-child relationships. But just how long is a generation? Is it still 20 years?

In recent years, it is a matter of common knowledge that a generation averages about 25 years from the birth of a parent to the birth of a child, even though in specifics, it varies case by case. Yes, admittedly this was closer to 20 years in earlier times when humans mated younger and life expectancies were shorter? In this brief example, we can certainly conclude that the term generation as a term that depicts the passing of time is a moving target that today is somewhere between twenty and twenty-five years and as time goes by, we can expect that to change.

Today, it is not good enough to refer to generations as time periods as most people when discussing generations have a specific starting period and ending period, of which they are interested. And so, we find terms such as "Gen X," "Baby Boomer", "The Greatest Generation, and others to refer to specific generations, all of which represent periods that are in the neighborhood of twenty to twenty-five years in duration, though even this is not a hard rule.

It can be argued that these phrases, used in the lingo of today, come from the larger discipline of demographics, and are used most frequently by market researchers, looking for a theoretically simple, one or two-word phrase to capture the notion of a particular age grouping. Most often such phrases are developed by companies so that sales campaigns can be directed towards specific groups. However, more and more people if not mostly everybody today has begun to use the words for various generations and sub-generations to avoid appearing dumb.

These cue words or phrases for the subcomponents of society are mainly demarcated by age and thus, they are not only useful, but are generally the language used by non-demographers (you and I) and society as a whole when discussing the current spectrum of population cohorts.

Because one cannot just begin talking about millennials without explaining what they are and where they fit, we begin this chapter and this book by providing this primer on the identification and description of the population cohorts in America as currently agreed upon by demographers and market researchers. However, even though most agree, this definition does not mean that this is the one source to which you can go to get the definitions. There are other sources and their definitions may not be exactly fit those shown in this chapter.

Let's start defining generations beginning with the turn of the twentieth century and go to definitions that exist today:

- ✓ Traditionalists or Silent Generation: Born 1945 & before
- ✓ Baby Boomers: Born 1946 to 1965
- ✓ Generation X: Born 1966 to 1976
- ✓ Millennials or Generation Y or Echo Boomers: Born 1977 to 1995
- ✓ Generation Z, iGen, or Centennials: Born 1996 & later

Traditionalists

The traditionalists or as some call them, the silent generation were born before 1945 and are subdivided by some into the following generations:

- • Depression Era Born 1912-1921.
- • World War II Era Born 1922 to 1927
- • Post War Cohort Born 1928 - 1944

Depression Era 1912-1921

Depression era individuals tend to be conservative, compulsive savers, maintain low debt and use more secure financial products like CDs versus stocks. These individuals tend to feel a responsibility to leave a legacy to their children. Tend to be patriotic, oriented toward work before pleasure, respect for authority, have a sense of moral obligation.

World War II 1922-1927

People in this cohort shared in a common goal of defeating the Axis powers. There was an accepted sense of "deferment" among this group, contrasted with the emphasis on "me" in more recent (i.e. Gen X) cohorts.

Post War Cohort 1928-1944

This sub-generation had significant opportunities in jobs and education as the War ended and a post-war economic boom overtook America. However, the growth in Cold War tensions, the potential for nuclear war and other never before seen threats led to levels of discomfort and uncertainty throughout the generation. Members of this group value security, comfort, and familiar, known activities and environments.

Baby Boomers

The Baby Boomers have also been subdivided in some research into the following generations:

- ✓ Boomers I Born 1946 – 1954
- ✓ Boomers II, aka Generation Jones Born 1955 – 1965

Baby Boomers I 1946-1954

For a long time, all Baby Boomers were defined as those born between 1945 and 1964. That would make the generation huge (71 million) and encompass people who were 20 years apart in age.

It did not make sense for those born in 1964 compared with those born in 1946. Life experiences were completely different. Attitudes, behaviors and society were vastly different.

In effect, all the elements that help to define a cohort were violated by the broad span of years originally included in the concept of the Baby Boomers. The first Boomer segment is bounded by the Kennedy and Martin Luther King assassinations, the Civil Rights movements and the Vietnam War. Boomers I were engaged in or they protested the War. Boomers 2 also called the Jones Generation missed the whole thing.

Boomers I had good economic opportunities and were largely optimistic about the potential for America and their own lives, the Vietnam War notwithstanding. The Vietnam War was very unsettling for all Americans but especially the Boomers I cohort.

Baby Boomers 2 1955-1965

This first post-Watergate generation lost much of its trust in government and the mostly optimistic views of the Boomers I generation. Economic struggles including the oil embargo of 1979

The events of the time reinforced a sense of "I'm out for me" and narcissism and a focus on self-help and skepticism over media and institutions. These are representative of attitudes of this cohort.

While Boomers I had Vietnam, Boomers II had AIDS as part of their rite of passage. The youngest members of the Boomer II generation in fact did not have the benefits of the Boomer I class as many of the best jobs, opportunities, housing etc. were taken by the larger and earlier group. Both Gen X and Boomer II folks suffer from this long shadow of opportunity lost by Boomers I.

Generation X 1966-1976

Sometimes referred to as the "lost" generation, this was the first generation of "latchkey" kids, exposed to lots of daycare and divorce. They are one generation removed from the Me-first generation. They are well known as the generation with the lowest voting participation rate of any generation ever.

Gen Xers were quoted by Newsweek as "the generation that dropped out without ever turning on the news or tuning in to the social issues around them." I know when we got an X-Genner at IBM, they were not thankful like we were to work for such a great company but instead were looking for something from the company without providing much in return.

Gen X is often characterized by high levels of skepticism, "what's in it for me" attitudes and a reputation for some of the worst music to ever gain popularity.

Now, moving into adulthood William Morrow (Generations) cited the childhood divorce of many Gen Xers as "one of the most decisive experiences influencing how Gen Xers will shape their own families". Gen Xers are arguably the best educated generation with 29% obtaining a bachelor's degree or higher (6% higher than the previous cohort).

And, with that education and a growing maturity, they are forming families with a higher level of caution and pragmatism than their parents demonstrated. Concerns run high over avoiding broken homes, kids growing up without a parent around and financial planning.

Generation Y, Echo Boomers or Millenniums 1977-1995

The largest cohort since the Baby Boomers, their high numbers reflect their births as that of their parent generation. The last of the Boomer I's and most of the Boomer II's. Gen Y kids are known as incredibly sophisticated, technology wise, immune to most traditional marketing and sales pitches…as they not only grew up with it all, they've seen it all and been exposed to it all since early childhood.

Gen Y members are much more racially and ethnically diverse and they are much more segmented as an audience aided by the rapid expansion in Cable TV channels, satellite radio, the Internet, e-zines, etc.

Gen Y are less brand loyal, and the speed of the Internet has led the cohort to be similarly flexible and changing in its fashion, style consciousness and where and how it communicates.

Gen Y kids often raised in dual income or single parent families have been more involved in family purchases…everything from groceries to new cars. One in nine Gen Yers has a credit card co-signed by a parent.

Generation Z 1996 and later

The Generation Z cohort have just begun to become young adults in recent years. We know a lot about the environment in which they grew up. This highly diverse environment is making the grade schools of the last defined generation the most diverse ever.

Higher levels of technology are making significant inroads in academics allowing for customized instruction, data mining of student histories to enable pinpoint diagnostics and remediation or accelerated achievement opportunities.

Gen Z kids are growing up with a highly sophisticated media and computer environment and are more Internet savvy and expert than their Gen Y, millennial forerunners. But, Millennials never admit not knowing anything about anything so we would never know from listening to them.

The end of the Millennial generation and the start of Gen Z in the United States are closely tied to September 11, 2001. That day marks the number-one generation-defining moment for

Millennials. Members of Gen Z—born in 1996 and after—cannot process the significance of 9/11 and it's always been a part of history for them. The research continues on all generations but Gen Z is just out the shoot so we will be getting even more interesting findings as time goes by.

Chapter 3 What is the Deal with Millennials?

Is there anything good about millennials?

No generation as a whole in history has ever been subject to the ridicule that is meted out to millennials on a daily basis.

Some say millennials deserve the put-downs and some say they don't. In the midst of all these put-downs of the "snowflake" generation, it sure seems one big fact has been lost: Millennials are people too! And, they are a lot nicer than most other people think.

That does not mean that they do not deserve the rap that they have gotten. Think about the story of the Yale Professor who had to give his suffering students an optional midterm because they were upset with Donald Trump's victory. Online comments about this were plentiful with the usual mocks about the snowflake generation, the spoiled, entitled babies, raised to love only themselves, coddled by their parents and adorned with participation trophies that everybody received.

Growing up in the age of social media made this generation obsessed with instant gratification. Things have gone bad for millennials as they reached adult-hood and even before. They need again the kind of great reinforcement that they had in T-Ball through adolescence when the participation trophies were the rage. Today, they get their kicks by being rewarded with online actions such as a "like" or "retweet." The US workplace was not ready for millennials and maybe that's why, so many are still unemployed. Of course, it might also be that foreign nationals took their jobs.

At work, if they can find a job, needy millennials like that feely-good stuff just like the social "likes" and "retweets." They'll even settle for constructive criticism if that's all a peer can muster but they would prefer lots of reinforcement or praise, especially from a manager. This need was not in their original genes; but the need seeped in as dose after dose, feely-good stuff was always the remedy. Even good dads had a hard time denying them.

Millennials are known as the selfish generation. It is said that they need to look up the meaning of the word, friend, each time somebody accuses them of being one. They are tarred with being the lazy and entitled generation, because from my observations, they often behave that way. Sometimes I wonder if I am the only one who sees it?

Maybe they have a really valid beef with life. Their generation is saddled with $1.45 billion in student loan debt. That would keep many smiles down. This book is written for the flawless millennials, so they can see their flaws as others see them and know why they have them. It is written for moms and dads and kindergarten teachers and lots of others, hoping that we never put out a group of participation trophy winners like this ever again. This author believes that being a millennial is not a terminal disease and the more the patient knows about herself, the easier the cure will be.

The millennial trick: only care about oneself

Young Americans are often lumped together under the term "millennials." One of the raps that stick on millennials is that they care about nobody but themselves and they are creating a new world order in which nobody cares about them. It is the ultimate karma. So far, it sure appears they deserve the rap.

As a group, they ought to be ashamed of themselves; but they will never admit shame. They know everything. Instead of reflection, they dig in against the thought of themselves not being perfect, while clutching their T-Ball participation trophy close to their hearts. The trophy is symbolic of the good-old days when simply breathing normally could bring a big participation award. As they reach adulthood, millennials become very disturbed about a new three-letter concept that they must endure that makes getting older not worth it –> J-O-B

These new Americans come in many shapes and sizes. Most can be recognized by their disrespect for their flag, their country, and their elders. They are empowered by the feelings they receive from those emotions. They feel that they have a right to everything anybody else possesses. After all, who else might be more deserving?

Compared with the world

An international study found America's millennials are lacking in major job skills areas such as literacy, problem solving, and job skills. This is a problem that participation trophies cannot help correct. And, that is why the proverbial problem with millennials will take a while to fix.

There is major irony in the discovery of this problem as there is no doubt that US millennials especially are the most educated and tech savvy generation of all in the U.S. Yet, millennials in the US, according to this study, are the world's least skilled people. That hurts but most Americans, especially Boomers, are aware there is some problem with millennials.

We are talking about a recent study by the Educational Testing Service (ETS) that demonstrates conclusively that America's millennials, on average, display weak skills in literacy, math and problem solving when compared to international competition. The study examined millennials from 22 countries, including the United States. It was part of the International Assessment of Adult Competencies Program.

The authors reported that the average scores for U.S. millennials were lower than in many other countries and that the U.S. ranked at the bottom in numeracy and PS-TRE. By the way, PS-TRE is defined as: "using digital technology, communication tools, and networks to acquire and evaluate information, communicate with others, and perform practical tasks. Considering it is a rare moment that millennials are seen without some digital device, the PS-TRE rating is very unexpected. I suspect the problem here is not understanding digital technology but communication.

The U.S. ranked first in just one area: In the study, it had the widest gap of any of the countries between the achievement of those in the top 10 percent and those in the bottom 10 percent of performance.

Seventy-two percent of young adults with a high school diploma or less did not meet minimum proficiency levels in numeracy. In fact, the top performing millennials in the U.S. scored lower than top-performing millennials in 15 of the 22 participating countries. Experts have thus concluded that this means that the US skills challenge is systemic.

Low-scoring U.S. millennials ranked last and scored lower than their peers in 19 participating countries. My personal analysis concludes that if there were not so many documented issues already with millennials in the US, experts would be taking issue with the validity of the testing and its possible bias towards the US in one way or another. The problem for America is that these test results are believable.

Millennials, Democracy & other American notions

As reported in The New York Times, one of the Young American's favorite rag, millennials, in particular, appear to be turning their backs on democracy. No kidding! Lots of things that my generation would simply dismiss is now the gospel understood by the younger generation.

The Baby Boomers' distaste for the lying Grey Lady has not reached our younger Americans who would give up Democracy in a heartbeat as they believe that army rule would be either "good" or "very good for the country." This statistic for those long in the tooth that is a planned bequeath to millennials rose to 1 in 6 in 2014. Compare this with 1 in 16 in 1995.

Whereas 43 percent of older Americans believe it is wrong for a military to take over even if government performs incompetently, only 19 percent of young Americans agreed. Millennials compared with the 60's generation are a definite anomaly.

They love the fake news media to pieces. They love believing lies and arguing points ad absurdum. They love liberal progressive coffee-breath professors who get them involved in great American activities such as protesting free speech and such. Isn't America great?

Millennials love the Democratic Party sometimes, but only the Bern factions, for providing them with encouragement through petty participation activities and trophies. Some are fully dedicated to gaining a lifetime participation trophy in the art of participation. However, few can make decisions and, so they have yet to choose an endeavor in which they wish to be recognized as participatory.

As some are beginning the aging process, though they won't admit it, they are pleased that the magazines on the rack at Dr. Bosley's (The Hair Guy) Office never show anything negative about life. More than ever, these young Americans as they progress in years find, themselves like us all, getting a little thin on the hair and thin on the tooth as they become long in the tooth. It's just as it is. They continue nonetheless to believe they need nothing that older generations needed because they are invincible.

Out of necessity, those who as undergraduates, took their coffee-breath professor's opinions to heart, have found that participation at free events such as the Soup Kitchens across America provides not only a new kind of rush, but they have found the experience is also very nourishing at the right price—free!

Despite how they measure their gains in life, they do wonder why anybody would give up a fun day in the sun or snow to work in such a kitchen; but the food is so darn good, they can't help coming back for more. They never give a thought as to where the food comes from as they have better things to think about such as their collective hate for the President.

We can bet they'll soon be standing in line if they begin to give out trophies for participation in anti-Trump rallies. It would be just like getting a participation trophy in the youth soccer league for the year in which they could not play because they were sick.

From my personal observations as they grow older, these young Americans, aka millennials, might even consider joining in on anti-American rallies if the promoters promised everybody the coveted participation trophies. Wow! Isn't life great!

Blame mom and dad first

Children do not reach the age of reason until seven years old, or so, we are told. So, we certainly cannot blame the diaper boy or the potty girl and that gets us to three or four, just about the age of competitive sports—and the still recent phenomenon, participation trophies.

So, at least until they were seven, millennials were not the biggest problem in their probable future demise. It was mom and dad for sure.

Since I have used this term a number of times in this book, let's find a definition for participation trophy. You probably already guessed it. Here is a definition from Wikipedia: "A participation trophy is a trophy given to children who participate in a sporting event but do not finish in first, second or third place, and so would not normally be eligible for a trophy. It is frequently associated with millennials."

There are a lot of moms and dads of theirs (the young American millennials) who have sucked up every word that ultra-lib Rachel

Maddow and her ilk have ever uttered. Looking around at their flawless junior and/or juniorettes, you can get a feeling about all the good the participation trophies really did for their families.

Moms and dads are ultimately responsible for junior and juniorette. I know my parents would leave the blame right there where it belongs. However, my mom and dad did not have to do so because they were their kids' teachers all our lives. I never wanted to cross my mom or dad, for example, because I loved them, and I respected them. They were part of that special generation and they worked hard to make sure the five siblings in my family were all OK. They also reached out and helped others.

Writing for AARP, The Magazine in 2016, Sally Koslow and Caity Weaver net it out quickly about "The Terrible 22's. I love the title:

Sorry, kids: we made you this way

"It's become a weary trope: Millennials, we are often told, are a pampered cohort sulking in their childhood bedrooms or aimlessly couch surfing in search of personal fulfillment. It's easy to get all judgy about the terrible 22s. But that's just part of the problem. What's truly terrible isn't our kids — it's us, the hyper-attentive parents who made them. Consider the oft-quoted profundity that parents should give children both roots and wings. We seem to have neglected *part two*.
…

"This generation is less able to perform in a tough world because of their high expectations about how easy things will be," says Jean Twenge, author of *Generation Me: Why Today's Young Americans Are More Confident, Assertive, Entitled — and More Miserable Than Ever Before*. We've put our children on a pedestal and given lots of praise without having rules. After such a childhood, reality hits like a smack in the face."

"Some parents never bothered to teach everyday life skills and assumed the role of concierge /personal assistant. We did this on purpose, says Mary Dell Harrington of the parenting blog Grown and Flown:

"Taking care of practical things — making doctors' appointments or buying gifts for family members—becomes a sneaky way for parents to maintain codependence." Our logic: If our kids manage well without us, that must mean we are old."

That is an indictment of millennial parents if I have ever read one. Thank you Sally, Caty, and the others.

The school district is not responsible for anybody's kids once they leave mom and dad. The parents are responsible. Great Kindergarten training can help; but great parents hold the keys to their children's future more than anybody else. I get the idea that moms and dad's worried about careers more than kids got us into the millennial caricature mess. Is it a caricature or is it reality is what is yet to be determined?

Unfortunately, today, even I, as a nationalist, populist, Trump-loving conservative, have no choice but to admit that there are many co-conspirators to the demise of American youth. Thus, what has happened to our young Americans cannot be dismissed as simple circumstance, or a death wish of the young. At the very least we know something went terribly wrong with a whole generation of Americans. We see it every day.

How about if we explore all these notions further. Let's review how our millennial young Americans have been left to form their negative opinions of America and their fellow Americans. Let's summarize a look from the time before they become young adults until the time they graduate from their college or university.

- ✓ 1 Moms and Dads who love liberalism and progressivism and socialism, forgot all their lessons and so all the juniors never had a chance.
- ✓ 2. Liberal / progressive coffee breath professors in universities have no shame nor love of truth.
- ✓ 3. Fake news from the finest liars in the universe seems real.
- ✓ 4. Democrats rooting against the good things in America can be convincing if they offer participation rewards.
- ✓ 5. Socialist / progressives who hate US Capitalism are on the liberal fake news channel all day long.

How my dad would have handled it.

My dad ruled our home with an iron fist. His Motto was "my wife is the master of this house…whatever she shall say shall be done." I can recall the thing in my life that made all else seem better. With a loving mom and grand mom, and a father that took no crap, my brothers and I got real lessons in life and my sisters got a lot of love. There were no spankings for my two sisters, who today, we call the Dolly Sisters. My brother and I when we crossed to the dark side, got the belt. Wow, did that sting! Let me assure you all, the offenses were few and far between and unlike millennials of today, the lesson was well learned.

One of my recent books requested that Congress and our new president solve the millennial crisis, which in that book was about all of the student debt that they owed. It is truly a sin that Congress by its action and inaction has cut a 20-year hole in American History. They have taken away many of the opportunities that would make millennials real people.

Young Americans, mostly millennials, suffered through a combination of bad parenting, short-lasting Kindergarten lessons, and a penchant for the liberal side. It has gotten worse. They are now literally choking on their student debt. Most should never have taken the loans. Nonetheless, the staggering student debt has their lives stopped. Studying the matter, the responsibility for this is directly related to a Congress that is not doing its job. Check out this book

https://www.amazon.com/dp/1947402234
Wipe Out All Student Loan Debt--Now!: Unique solutions to the $1.45 Trillion debt accumulation

Each year that this problem is not solved by Congress, is another year for many millennials in a veritable debtor's prison. It is so bad that 50% in a recent survey would be willing to give up their most fundamental freedom, the right to vote, to have their debt lifted and be able to lead a normal life. I do feel sorry for millennials in a lot of ways

Bruce Ritter, writing for The RealTruth.com discusses the rise of the millennials. Without even writing a word in the piece, Ritter captures the essence of the millennial in his subtitle: *Why They Know So Much…Yet Understand So Little.* Ritter notes:

" They are smart, resourceful, talented, highly educated, team-oriented and well-traveled. Yet the average Millennial does not know how to professionally conduct him or herself in the office. He lacks the training to use proper etiquette at business dinners and other special occasions. He was not taught to value the hands-on experience of older, more seasoned generations. And he does not know how and when to accept "no" for an answer."

Ritter sees some of these lifetime events as contributing factors that millennials have had to overcome. Consider the life-defining events that shaped their young lives:

* **The Columbine shooting**
* **The 9/11 attacks**
* **Corporate corruption scandals**
* **War on Terrorism**
* **Anti-Americanism**
* **A nuclear North Korea**
* **Emerging nations**
* **The "dot-com boom"**
* Pocket Electronics
* **Hurricane Katrina**
* Lots of others

With all of this baggage, millennials are not being excused by the world. They are cocky and pompous and many seem lazy. They look like they walk like they own the world.

They know it all from all the parenting and life guidance mistakes to which they were subjected. Yet, they feel no need for correction, and that is their biggest problem today. There is no fix for anyone unwilling to listen to the fix. They need a special treatment like AA to get them out of their funk or they will be the missing generation in US history.

Nobody was ever able to tell them what to do and so they never saw a need to listen and they still do not listen. Even today, when they are hurting, they place the blame in the wrong places and they cling to liberal progressive and hateful ideals that are more harmful that the poor lessons of their early lives.

For Boomers, the millennials of today serve the same role as President Trump does for Never-Trumpers. There has to be somebody that we can set up as the bad guy. Millennials are not that bad and should not be punished by America, but then again, neither should President Trump. When we fix that part of our culture, we will all be better off. Perhaps we will all, with the help of millennials who are in many ways are MIA, we will be able to reclaim an entire generation of human beings. Let's hope we can.

No, we should not deport them, but sometimes they make us feel like we would if we could. In the meantime, it would help reduce their opportunity for deportation if they stopped following goofy Governors such as Andrew Cuomo, and Jerry "Moonbeam" Brown.

Chapter 4 Conservatives Are Mad as Hell re: Leftist Dominated Media!

I'm Mad as Hell!

Conservatives do not need a census to know that most reporters and editors are liberal. There is a one-time Pew Research Center poll that found that liberals outnumber conservatives in the media by some 5 to 1, and that is lower than I would conclude from my own experience. It gets to you when every thought you hear is liberal and mostly untrue. However, for liberals, when everyone else around you as you write the news is a liberal, it is easy to be sucked into the chasm of groupthink on what stories are important, what sources are legitimate and what the narrative of the day should be. For conservatives, whatever they choose to write is going to make us mad as hell.

Millennials are in a league of their own, but they are easily influenced by liberal groupthink and the thoughts of winning another big participation trophy. So, they typically line up on the liberal lefty side of the ledger. The lefties have a deep concern that is spurred by a fear that red and blue America are drifting irrevocably apart and their side is not going to dominate.

The corrupt mainstream media has decided to be a branch of the leftist Democratic Party and that its mission is to remove President Donald Trump from Office and the quicker the better. They don't really care whether America was or is great as long as nobody can credit Trump with making it great. Fake news and outright lies are the media weapons of choice and they have a huge following of lefty-type people, including millennials who have been enjoying their work in trying to depose our president one way or another.

Though most Americans are not privileged, the media and the Democratic leadership and a large part of the Republican Establishment enjoy the fruits of political greed and the full benefits of the "Swamp." It's been like that for too many years to expect that anything, the purpose of which is the good of the country, would have any meaning to them.

The daily soap opera promulgated by this nasty press every day spews vile on the President and tries to convince weak-minded Americans that by jumping on their negative train they can gain back the great times from the last eight great Obama years. The press is actually worse than the far left in trying to persuade Americans to give up the Constitution and bring in a socialist regime.

Fixthisnation.com began their explanation for a new White House set of talking points intended to fight the fake news and it is the perfect way to begin this book about whether or not America was ever great. Why? Because like everything including the fake *Russia collusion soap opera*, the press tells one fat lie after another. So far, other than lefties, Americans are not buying it and that is good.

"The White House often issues talking points to allies in the Republican Party– talking points that are almost certainly going to be ignored by politicians who refuse to stand up to the media's ideological tyranny. As far as the mainstream right is concerned, President Trump is completely toxic at this point. Like rats from a sinking ship, Republicans of the "Never Trump" variety are doing everything they can to distance themselves from the president, as if he REALLY IS the neo-Nazi, white supremacist that the liberal media insists that he is. It occurs to only a very, very select few that maybe – just maybe – it's just the media lying once again in an attempt to smear all of conservatism with the same racist brush."

"The president, said one set of issued talking points, were "entirely correct – both sides of the violence in Charlottesville acted inappropriately, and bear some responsibility." The memo went on to encourage Republicans to remind the press that Trump used "no ambiguity" in condemning the white supremacist groups that gathered for the rally at UVA and in the Town Square the next day. The White House asked allies to present President Trump as "a voice for unity and calm" and a leader "taking swift action to hold violent hate groups accountable." "

As Americans have begun to discern, the press is not only anti-Trump, they are anti-American, and they lie like the Devil to try to suck in weaker Americans, especially fragile millennials, into their doomsday party. Many Americans simply can't take it anymore.

I can't take it anymore

Do you remember back in November 1976 when Howard Beale, as played by Peter Finch, the long-time anchor in the movie "Network News," gets the bad news that eventually causes him to utter one of the most famous movie lines of all time? Beale gets fired and is given two weeks. The long-time anchor has a very poor reaction to this personal news and he cannot control himself during the next broadcast. He "goes off the deep end."

He promises to commit suicide on the air. The company immediately fires him—no second chances for a repeat performance. Beale is devastated and remorseful. He begs for the opportunity to say good-by to his fans with dignity, and he is given his last opportunity ever for air time so that he can say his good-by's respectfully and also apologize. Nobody expects it to happen, but Beale gets his chance, and it is billed as a last chance.

Despite his promises, once on the air, Beale is overwhelmed by his circumstance. He goes into another diatribe starting off with a rant claiming that "Life is bullshit." He is so passionate that his ratings spike as he persuades his viewers to shout out of their windows: "I'm as mad as hell, and I'm not going to take this anymore!" Like the shot at Lexington and Concord, this is the line heard round the world.

Well, my fellow Americans, I bet you saw this coming, and I am going to deliver it as passionately in words as I can: "I am mad as hell, and I am not going to take this anymore." I bet you are too. Let me remind you of why you are upset.

If you read the Preface, you may find some of this redundant but many do not believe that America suffers so please hear those parts again. Taxes are too high, elected officials are out of touch, government is too big, spending is out of control, the Obamacare program has been a train wreck from its inception, and heroes are dying in the VA system,

The people see the federal government as incompetent and the left wing news outlets as purposely failing to report the truth about the corrupt and incompetent government. We the common citizens have no voice in our own government; too many people are too lazy to hold government accountable, and too many of our finest are on the take. Only you and I can bring this back to being OK, but not by sitting on our duffs.

Our country run by this government is a train wreck and when they ran in 2016, Hillary Clinton, and Bernie Sanders promised to keep the train derailed for another eight years. They loved how things were. The people did not like it and that is why our President is now Donald J. Trump.

Corporate leaches and leakers have infiltrated our government. We have record unemployment while illegal aliens are smiling as they take American jobs. We have an unsustainable status quo with special interests having priority over the people's interests. When we look to the future we see a public education system that creates more dummies than smart people. These dummies are so dumb that they don't seem to mind being called dummies. Scrooge could have come up with an even more devastating term than "Bah Humbug." It's that bad! Can't you feel it?

Before Trump began putting us on the right track, we had the poorest economy since the depression with excessive welfare and income redistribution, institutionalized lying, a corrupt press carrying water for government, a debt large enough to kill America, huge student debt stopping graduate's success, tyranny v. democracy, government lawlessness, freedom and liberty in jeopardy, American stagnation, and a big loss of American world prestige.

Why we do not regularly hear about this is because we have the most corrupt press since Gutenberg finally got his mechanical printing invention working. The American media in all forms works hard to propagandize all aspects of American life while championing the liberal leftist progressive wing of the Marxist / Communist oriented new Democratic Party.

Our big government has become such a problem that it can never again be the solution. Our finest hope, our youth; go through colleges with socialist / communist administrators and professors in huge numbers to ultimately become unemployed and sacked with debt. Their out of touch coffee-breath professors have convinced them that this is the norm though their parents sent them to school because they believed that the American Dream was the norm. It was. But, no longer! Today's millennials do not believe in the American Dream or any dreams because their elitist professors hate America and they lecture accordingly.

The student loan burden prevents borrowers from buying homes, cars, and having a family. As many as 37 million student loan borrowers are too broke to engage in life. College loans, instead of lifting people to the top, have created a new race to the bottom,

On the International stage, thanks to our elected government, America for the last eight years was known as a bad actor. Nobody gives America a standing ovation anymore. Nobody asks us for curtain calls. Our leaders have turned their backs on our friends and they pay homage to our enemies.

Nightclubs in Orlando create major carnage while, so as not to offend the new religion of acceptability in the US, the government blames Christians and guns rather than the work of an ISIS terrorist, the hate mongering perpetrators of the atrocity. A church is attacked by a deranged killer in Texas and Democrats don't want to hear that he lied about his dishonorable discharge and under current law should not have been permitted to buy any gun. Why not try to treat people who are mentally sick?

Before Trump, smaller and weaker countries such as Russia, Iran, and North Korea pushed US around and laughed at US, and our only response was to see if somehow, we may have offended them. For me, these have been the worst days of America that I have ever witnessed, and the leadership and our government (other than the new president who does give us all hope) seem to be OK with being mediocre, instead of being outstanding. Our elected government has trained us not to fight the bad guys. Wimps and pure traitors from the Swamp control the Congress

If you have been paying attention, and I sure hope you have been as it is a civic duty, you know that there are even more issues than the exhaustive list we just walked through. Isn't that a shame on US? I think that is why you bought this book. Thank you very much.

We are on the same side, and together we can all help. We first must understand what is going on and we then must understand our rights. Even before you and me and everybody else are on board, we must start the first wave of solutions by opening our windows all the way and shouting as loud as we can so all of the government perpetrators in Washington can hear us well: "I am mad as hell, and I am not going to take this anymore."

Then, we must make sure that we talk to everybody we can out there that we know—other people like you and I and others, and let's help them know that unless we all fully engage in America, when we wake up from our deep fog, there may be no America left for our progeny. We will have blown it for sure.

Chapter 5 America is a Representative Democracy?

The United States of America – a Representative Democracy
- We have representatives to speak for us at all levels.
- City Councils, County Councils, State Governments, and also the men and women that we elect to represent us in Washington, DC.

The USA is more a Republic

Civics and anything about the goodness of America are no longer taught in our schools. Consequently, millennials have no idea if America ever was great. Moreover, the corrupt media with its members practicing on the left side all the time, tells them every day that Trump is not going to make it any greater despite his promises. So, when things are improving because of decreased regulations and more money in taxpayers' pockets the media continues to poor mouth the country and gives no credit to Trump for what most economists see as purely spectacular results. It is enough to make an honest person mad.

If you were in a position to rebel against an oppressive handler, say England in the seventeenth century, what type of government would you form to make sure you would gain freedom and stay free. Suppose you and a number of cohorts orchestrated a Declaration of Independence and you fought a revolution for your freedom against this oppressive regime. Again, what type of government would you establish so that you had a say in what happened and the new government was supported by the rule of law.

This is exactly what the founders faced after winning a major war against an oppressive English nation. History provides many examples from the Romans and Greeks through time to England herself. All forms of governments from dictatorial to Democracies have advantages. But which is best? The founders decided that the people needed a voice but there had to be rules.

And, so the government type that was fostered was called a Republic, which many refer to as a Constitutional Democracy. This has all the advantages of a democracy plus it has a bunch of rules as tie breakers for when the goodness of the representatives was directed for self-serving purposes rather than for the people. The US Republic is based on the best form of government known at the time. The founders could not have selected a better form. Think of a representative government with a Constitution and that about describes the government of the USA

When we think of the very important notion that "America is a representative democracy," watching the clowns who occupy our central government today, it is a sane question to ask if this is really true. The song, "Is that all there is?" comes to mind today. We are nothing like our parents and nothing like our founders. We should all be ashamed but then again shame is no longer permitted.

A representative democracy is the foundation of America. However, what makes America, America is that we are also a Republic, the finest form of government ever brought forth from the smartest people in mankind.

We also have a set of laws, beginning with our Constitution that govern all politicians in perpetuity—as long as we hold them accountable. Our government has gotten away from us in recent times, because the people have not been brave enough to use the Constitution to reign in rogue actors who are not interested in what is best for the people.

The big laws like the Constitution are not so that the government can hurt us or impose its will upon US. Not hardly! Our country was founded by some smart people and they knew that without constraints on government gone wild, such as a great body of law known as the Constitution, politicians and others in government would feel they had a right to deny US our liberty and freedom. They are trying real hard today to kill America, so you are reading this book none too soon.

If you could figure any way to put a stranglehold on corrupt politicians, right now or in the future, would you not do it? The founders of America put such a stranglehold on all political agents of the future when they wrote and adopted the US Constitution, the greatest body of law ever written in any civilization.

Of course, if we the people do not know what is written in the Constitution, it can't help us much. Can it? So, it is time to stop being dummies and political sport for the elite. It is time to rule America as our birthright as citizens of this great country commands US. Let somebody else eat cake!

And, so, my fellow Americans, that is the number one reason that in order to form a more perfect union of the thirteen colonies / states, and with many more states expected, our forefathers built the finest Constitution ever fashioned by the pen of human beings.

Our former President Obama bragged about having a pen and a phone, but he did not have much else. His pen and his phone worked against the Law of the Land, not to assure its execution. His pen and phone could not work the magic of the founders. Apparently, though he taught Constitutional Law, he did not seem to understand its principles, or he was not interested in trying to uphold the most basic law of America.

The Bible, from the hand of God, may be the greatest story ever told in the greatest book ever written, but the Constitution is as good as it gets for the goodness of man, written by the hands of our first patriots, and surely this was with the guidance of God.

In this day and age, there are everyday attempts by the government to undermine our lasting Republic, which is an almost pure constitutional representative democracy. The attacks most often come from the left side of the political spectrum.

The ideology of the progressive left favors Marxism and its simpler forms of socialism and communism. Since Americans do not vote for socialists, communists, or Marxists, these are things that nobody other than a crooked politician would want. If we are unaware of this in today's government, it is time we all paid more attention. No politician wanting to be elected will admit they are more communist than American. Yet, as much as it pains me to tell you, they are!

These overtures, which demean the Constitution, the fabric of our democracy, originate from corrupt politicians who have been caught up in the leftist movement, which would like to end capitalism, and bring on a socialist order to replace the American Dream, and all the dreams of We the People!

One midnight, I asked myself one of those haunting questions: "Isn't it about time that we real Americans actually had some real "representation" from the so-called representatives in our so-called representative government? I said to myself: "Yes, it is!" It doesn't have to be a dream. If we believe, it can easily again be made a reality.

The way it now works provides far too much separation between US, the electors, and them, the elected officials who coordinate our pooled resources for the alleged benefit of "everyone." But who is everyone? And who takes credit for everything?

Do our representatives in the second decade of the twenty-first century have a genuinely compelling concern for the people and our government or is this simply a Nirvana, which in Buddhism is its final goal—a transcendent state in which there is neither suffering, desire, nor sense of self, and the subject is released from the effects of karma and the cycle of death and rebirth. If not Nirvana, perhaps it is a Disney-like Utopian myth perpetrated on US by these same "benevolent politicians?" Do any of US think they care?

I propose the latter. Our government is wholly unaccountable to We the People. Today, our government rejects the fundamental principles of our founding and has no real legitimacy the further it drifts from the precepts of the Constitution. We have a well-meaning President today, Donald J. Trump, and I believe God gave him to us to help us turn our country around.

But our representatives on both the Democratic side and the Republican side do not like this fine President, and they are working to undermine the people, the President, and the results of the last election. The people must replace these corrupt representatives to get a Congress that supports our wishes. That will help make America great again!

The US was not designed this way. It was designed by a group of artisans to not only represent their artistic touch, but to be held as the creed of the people, for the people, and by the people, forever. What thinking human being blessed to be part of America, could ask for anything more? But we must remember there are evil men who gain office and do not do their jobs.

If you think that life, freedom, liberty, and the ability to pursue your own happiness are simple notions, and *givens* in any civilization, get out your thinking pad, and think again. Why do people from all over the world crash our gates just to get in? It is because America has always been a great country, not as millennials and Andrew Cuomo and other Democrats would have us believe.

Which would you first give up? Your freedom, your life, your liberty, or your ability to do what you need to be happy? Who could ask for anything more than being an American? But, if Americans do not care about the great gift of God which is this country, maybe it cannot last.

If this design, which the founders labored to create for America was so great, you might ask, why is it that our current lawmakers ignore it? They have no trouble going with the flow and committing US to years of debt without even taking the time to read the debt-ridden legislation for which they vote.

Even worse, its members, our alleged civil servants, are able to get away without doing their jobs, while collecting more and more remuneration for the act of hurting the American people at large.

The true answer to that question is very unfortunate for Americans. There is tacit collaboration in undermining the principles of our Democratic Republic by our supposed representatives, their supporters, the special interests, and their corporate interests. We the people now come last. They think we are not paying attention.

Maybe we have not been paying enough attention, but don't you agree that is about to end. *Pay attention* is about to become the motto of the free! A group of Americans in Thirty States in our great Republic saw fit to elect Donald Trump as our 45th US President. He is doing his part to keep us free and prosperous. Now, it is time to give him a Congress that will do the work of the people.

Perhaps too many of US, until things got this bad, had been hoping George would do it! Well, George Washington, one of our finest patriots is long gone, and unless you know of a recent George with the time, it is up to US, each and every one of US, to do it.

And, by the way, the two George Bush's did not get it done either. And now, neither choose to be good Americans by supporting today's President, Donald Trump. I can't figure out how they supported Obama 100% for eight years as loyal Republicans It makes no sense to me.

When the Bushes were in charge, Americans were the least we could be but not as small as in the BHO years. Maybe the Bushes were not so bad after all. Maybe they were and still are. They could have done more but they did not cause today's morose outlook about life in America. BHO, for eight years of Obama baseball could step up to the plate and claim that all for himself. That in many ways is why Trump is now our President. Why the Bushes who we all once thought were patriotic cannot accept the new President places them right smack dab in the middle of the SWAMP. Whooda thunk?

To repeat the notion of our morose country needing a jolt to move forward. Remember that is what Trump is trying to do. I am proud of his efforts because I voted for him and despite having obstacle after obstacle placed in front of him, he gets up each morning and works for us to make America better.

Morose is not the color of America. Nor are a lot of other words / phrases for morose such as sullen, sulky, gloomy, bad-tempered, ill-tempered, dour, surly, sour, glum, moody, ill-humored, melancholy, melancholic, brooding, broody, doleful, miserable, depressed, dejected, despondent, downcast, unhappy, low, down, grumpy, irritable, churlish, cantankerous, crotchety, cross, crabby, cranky, grouchy, testy, snappish, peevish, crusty, etc. You get my drift.

Can it be that too many of US and too many of our friends have been constitutional dummies for too long? Perhaps this book and your exhortations to all your friends will help many Americans, especially millennials and those who like Andrew Cuomo, to awaken to what happens in a country in which government, rather than the people, has the stronger hand.

By the way, as much as they could have helped and did not do such a good job; the Bushes did not cause this problem. It rests on the shoulders of BHO. Yet, nobody in the 4th Estate wants to blame him for it, because he seems so happy messing with US all in his new resistance! Do you feel the same?

Chapter 6 Americans Benefit from Our Democratic Republic

As Benjamin Franklin was exiting after writing the U.S. constitution, a woman asked him, "Well, Doctor, what have we got—a republic or a monarchy?". He replied, "A republic—if you can keep it."

Nothing in life worth having, is easy

Our Constitutional Representative Democracy, aka, our Republic comes from the hard-fought battles of the Revolutionary War plus the craft of our founders in writing our country's original laws. Everything America was and is, is because of the work of the great men and women—the founders, who came before US. They were good people no matter what the faux preacher Andrew Cuomo has to say about America. What does he know?

Most Americans have a great feel for the notion of representative democracy and the sense that we elect representatives of the community to handle our affairs in the governing of the nation. We also have the privilege of a Constitution which is intended to prevent tyranny by a government gone wild. We do not have a direct democracy in that we do not conduct the activities of government ourselves in Washington.

It would be very difficult squeezing over 325 million people into a room in Washington D.C. Instead, we choose representatives among us to get the job done.

When you go through this whole book, your opinion of the purity of the act of representation may become tainted. That is OK. It should as corrupt politicians have made it so. I hope to generate some alarm and a sense of urgency among the readers for we simply may not have much time to get it right again.

Andrew Cuomo may say America was never great and that is not true, but it cannot ever achieve major greatness again as long as the likes of Andrew Cuomo vote against America and disrespect he when they have the obligation to make America a great place to live.

Something surely went wrong with the intention of representation from the Founding Fathers to what representation means today. Something went way wrong sometime between 1492 and the present day but the evidence suggests that the problem began closer to the year 2000 than to the year 1400. That's not to say that all was hunky-dory in the 1400s and onward. Let's jump from the 1400s to the mid to late 1700s to see how our government was formed. Today's leftists such as Andrew Cuomo as well as our corrupt mainstream press seem hell-bent on removing the foundations of America. We cannot let this happen.

The Formation of the United States Government

Representation at All Levels

As you know, governments do not appear out of thin air. They are crafted by mostly brilliant men and women. One of the first documents on the way to the Declaration of Independence and the Constitution in the formation of the United States of America was a short document known as the *Declaration of Rights and Grievances.* This was a product of the First Continental Congress.

At the First Continental Congress, the delegates drafted several documents, and several drafts of documents, one of these, the first, was the *Declaration of Rights and Grievances.* This was a statement of

American complaints as can be deduced by the title. It was sent to King George III, to whom, at the time, many of the delegates remained loyal. It was not sent to Parliament since the delegates did not have the same level of loyalty to this body. Quite frankly, the document implored King George III to step in and rescue the colonies from the English Parliament.

Though it was nothing close to a constitutional democracy, the Colonists under English rule enjoyed representation in the lower house of the colonial governments. There was no union of colonies or states at the time and perhaps if the English had kept to themselves and not levied taxes directly on the colonists, Americans today would be much more interested if Camilla is really ever going to be the Queen.

With a careful reading of the Declaration of Rights and Grievances, one can get a quick sense of what the colonists wanted from the Crown. It was simply, "no taxation without representation," and all of the many positions this plea represented. As the thought of a revolution became more of a reality for the Patriots, independence and freedom and liberty become even more important than the tax burden.

This early declaration was the first major document of the new government of the United States, though it occurred at a time when the states were not actively seeking independence from the Crown.

The expressed purpose of the First Continental Congress held in 1774 was:

> *"That a Committee be appointed to state the rights of the Colonies in general, the several instances in which these rights are violated or infringed, and the means most proper to be pursued for obtaining a restoration of them."*

The committee was constructed, and the declaration was drafted and it was read on September 22nd and the draft of the grievances was read on the 24th. The members of the First Congress debated the drafts on October 12 and 13, and after a final draft was produced, it was agreed on Friday, October 14, 1774.

Several days later on October 20, the Congress passed the Articles of Association. It was addressed to King George III. In essence, it was a formal agreement of the colonies themselves to work together as an association of states with common purpose. It was basically a union of protest and boycott as many of the articles outlined the specific actions that the colonists were to take regarding the export and import of goods.

All of the founding documents are readable for free on the Internet. Just type the name of the document into your search engine and it will be available to read for free. In Brian Kelly's book, Taxation Without Representation, all of these original documents are included in Appendices.

As you read these articles, you can't help but notice the elegance and forethought in the drafts. We are a fortunate lot indeed to have had such fine and capable, and yes, honorable men and women, representing America in those days. America was great in its founding, indeed!

Since life had not improved and the British, after initially backing off from its impositions, began to double down, continuing to impose its will on the colonists, The Second Continental Congress began on May 10, 1775 and it went on until March 1, 1781. During the war, the meeting location was moved from Philadelphia several times to other locations to protect the lives of the representatives.

The delegates of each of the 13 colonies gathered initially in Philadelphia to discuss their next steps in dealing with England. This Congress met at the State House in Philadelphia as the American Revolution had already begun in earnest with the shot heard round the world still ringing in their ears.

The militia was still engaged in Boston while the Congress was using its powers to formally establish the militia as the Continental Army of the United States with George Washington as the top general known at the time as the Commander in Chief. This marked another stage in the formation of the government of the US. The government would continue to evolve and after independence was gained, Washington would again become Commander in Chief when he was elected First President of the United States.

Sixty-five representatives originally appointed by the legislatures of thirteen British North American colonies accomplished a body of work that is historic in nature. At the time, it formed the basis for the new government. The Declaration of Independence, written by Thomas Jefferson, was the first well-known historic document produced by this Second Congress. The second was the Articles of Confederation, which served as the first "Law of the Land." This was the pre-cursor document to the United States Constitution.

As noted previously, the Second Continental Congress was begun during the American Revolutionary War. It served as the de facto U.S. national government. This Congress assumed power and raised armies, directed strategy, appointed diplomats, and it made the government formal.

At the same time, it produced numerous important documents, including three of the most fundamental and historic documents regarding American freedom—The Declaration of Independence, The Articles of Confederation, and The Constitution.

United States Declaration of Independence

Some dates, one can never forget. The Declaration of Independence was written by Thomas Jefferson, and it was put forth and approved for printing on July 4, 1776. It did exactly what it purported to do in its title. It declared independence from Great Britain.

It was not Pennsylvania, or Massachusetts or Virginia that declared this independence and this is a key point. Instead, it was all of the thirteen colonies in unison, known to themselves as states at the time. They had chosen to assemble and join in a union to create a new federal government that would be known as the United States of America.

Once independence was declared, America began to legally operate fully independent of the Crown with its own government. Considering that the colonists were in revolt and war had commenced, it is an understatement to suggest that the colonists were not operating independently prior to the Declaration. The Declaration formalized their union of independence.

The states were declared to be free and independent and "all political connection between them and the State of Great Britain, is and ought to be totally dissolved."

In addition to declaring independence, this document gave justification for the separation from the Crown in sufficient detail that the King and Parliament could not misunderstand its purpose and from whence it came. Since the colonies were no more, historians consider this Declaration as the founding document of the United States of America. In his Gettysburg Address of 1863, at the beginning of his address, President Lincoln memorialized the founding of the United States in these words:

> *Four score and seven years ago our fathers brought forth on this continent, a new nation, conceived in liberty, and dedicated to the proposition that all men are created equal.*

As we know from our knowledge of American History and from any recount of the Revolutionary War, there were a number of battles until the Americans prevailed in the war with England. After the *Declaration of Independence*, the Second Continental Congress stayed in session passing laws and drafting documents that ultimately would define the new nation as the United States of America. The next major document in the formation of the government of the United is known as *The Articles of Confederation.*

Articles of Confederation

Some say that the Articles of Confederation represent the United States of America's first Constitution. This document was the work of the Second Continental Congress, who drafted it in 1777. The Articles established a "firm league of friendship" between and among the 13 states.

After having been subjected to the wiles of the strong central government of the British prior to the War of Independence, these Articles reflect a sense of the wariness by the states of a government that would not provide them with their God-given rights.

The Articles are the agreed-upon remedy for the concerns of states' rights and for individual rights. Ever fearful that a government of the future (such as the regime from 2009 through 2016, or one hence) might not have the right measure of concern for our individual needs if it were given too much power, and that abuses such as the Intolerable Acts, might again be the result, the Articles purposely established a "constitution."

This document vested the largest share of power to the individual states. When the actual Constitution was built and later enacted, it reflected the same notion of states' rights and individual rights, as the Articles, and the last claimant on the rights list was the federal government in Washington. In other words the people ran the government. The government did not run the people. Does that not sound like a refreshing idea for a great country with a great founding.

Under the Articles of Confederation, each of the states retained its "sovereignty, freedom and independence." The preamble of the US Constitution drafted in 1787 and ratified later by the individual states one at a time, sets its purpose as "in order to form a more perfect union."

The founders of our government recognized that there were flaws in the Articles of Confederation that would more easily permit a tyranny to take place. And, so their best, "more perfect" work, the Constitution, was its way of correcting those flaws and correcting the notion of a constitutional representative democracy (aka, a Republic) for the United States.

There was a permanent institution called the Congress formed in the Articles as a national legislature comprised of representatives of the states. The Congress was responsible for conducting foreign affairs, declaring war or peace, maintaining an army and navy and a variety of other lesser functions.

The Articles did not call for the separation of powers with an executive, legislative, and judicial branch. The Articles did not permit the delegates to collect taxes, regulate interstate commerce and enforce laws. Under the Articles of Confederation these important functions could only be performed if the states chose to agree.

Though the Articles had shortcomings, the document provided the guidelines for the United States government and it was the only real law of the land until the Constitution was written, adopted and ratified.

Eventually, the shortcomings were addressed, and this led to the U.S. Constitution. The beauty of the Articles of Confederation was that it provided a workable framework during those years in which the 13 states were struggling to achieve their independent from Great Britain and their collective status.

Considering that the Constitution itself is under fire today by those who would like it constructed in ways that were not intended by the Founding Fathers, from November 15,1777, when adopted by the Congress, the Articles of Confederation did its job to keep the Country in good stead. Nothing in life worth having is easy.

On March1, 1781, the Articles became operational when the last of the thirteen states signed the document. Then came the work for the Constitution.

The Constitution

The Articles were an imperfect constitution for the newly formed union. The phrase "a more perfect union" in the Preamble notes the imperfections in the document and it introduces the rationale for the drawing of the Constitution.

The U.S. Constitution (and its subsequent 27 amendments) has survived for over two-hundred years testifying to its perfection as the basis for the constitutional representative democracy (Republic) of the United States.

From the National Archives:
http://www.archives.gov/national-archives-experience/charters/constitution.html

I like how this text from the national archives reads so instead of trying to rephrase this, I simply include it below to explain the purpose of the work behind the Constitution.

The Federal Convention convened in the State House (Independence Hall) in Philadelphia on May 14, 1787, to revise the Articles of Confederation. Because the delegations from only two states were at first present, the members adjourned from day to day until a quorum of seven states was obtained on May 25. Through discussion and debate it became clear by mid-June that, rather than amend the existing Articles, the Convention would draft an entirely new frame of government.

All through the summer, in closed sessions, the delegates debated, and redrafted the articles of the new Constitution. Among the chief points at issue were how much power to allow the central government, how many representatives in Congress to allow each state, and how these representatives should be elected--directly by the people or by the state legislators. The work of many minds, the Constitution stands as a model of cooperative statesmanship and the art of compromise.

The Law of the Land

As noted previously, the Constitution of the United States comprises the primary law of the U.S. Federal Government. In simple terms, it is the law of the land and all other laws must conform to the statutes with this original document and its amendments (changes).

It also describes the three chief branches of the Federal Government and their jurisdictions as well as the separation of the powers. In addition, it lays out the basic rights of citizens of the United States. The Constitution of the United States is the oldest federal constitution in existence and was framed by a convention of delegates from twelve of the thirteen original states in Philadelphia in May 1787.

The Constitution is the landmark legal document of the United States and all other laws are tested against its specifications. Many other constitutions, such as the Constitution of Mexico, for example are based on this work.

The full Constitution includes The Bill of Rights (first ten amendments) and the other 17 amendments. To give the reader an appreciation or a reminder of just how significant the Articles and the Amendments of this document really are, I am including this brief summary below:

Preamble

We the People of the United States, in Order to form a more perfect Union, establish Justice, insure domestic Tranquility, provide for the common defense, promote the general Welfare, and secure the Blessings of Liberty to ourselves and our Posterity, do ordain and establish this Constitution for the United States of America.

Article I: The Legislative Branch: Consists of 10 sections and defines:

(1) All Legislative powers, (2) Composition of the House of Representatives, (3) Composition of the Senate, (4) Holding Elections, (5) Congress sets its own rules by House, (6) Compensation for Senators), (7) Revenue Bills originate in House, (8) Congress can lay and collect taxes, (9) Defines states' rights and taxes (10) State treaties.

Section 9, Clause 8 of the Constitution is of particular interest to this writer. In later chapters, we discuss the automatic conferring of the title, the Honorable. Please look at what the founding fathers thought of such titles:

> *Section 9 Clause 8: No Title of Nobility shall be granted by the United States: And no Person holding any Office of Profit or Trust under them, shall, without the Consent of the Congress, accept of any present, Emolument, Office, or Title, of any kind whatever, from any King, Prince, or foreign State.*

One of the first constitutional loopholes was the notion of the giver being the King, Prince, or a foreign state. There is nothing here unfortunately about taking the title ("Honorable") for oneself or having it granted via obscure rules of etiquette that have never passed the test of law.

Article II: The Executive Branch: Consists of 4 sections and defines:

(1) Executive Power and President, (2) President as Commander in Chief, (3) State of the Union & Information Requirements, (4) Rules of Executive Branch impeachment

Article III: The Judicial Branch: Consists of 3 sections and defines:
(1) Judicial Power, (2) Laws and Trial by Jury, (3) Treason

Article IV: Relations Between States: Consists of 4 sections and defines:
(1) Faith and Credit of State Laws, (2) Privileges apply to all in all states, (3) New States May be Admitted to the Union, (4) Federal guarantee to defend states.

Article V: The Amendment Process:
Consists of 1 section and defines the Amendment Process for adding / deleting from the Constitution.

Article VI: General Provisions, Supremacy of the Constitution:
Consists of 1 section and defines the debt process and the requirement to support the Constitution

Article VII: Ratification Process:
Consists of 1 section and it outlines the process for ratifying the Constitution

27 Amendments to the Constitution

The Bill of Rights

Amendment I: Freedom of speech, religion, press, petition, assembly.
Amendment II: Right to bear arms and militia.
Amendment III: Quartering of soldiers.
Amendment IV: Warrants and searches.
Amendment V: Individual debt and double jeopardy.
Amendment VI: Speedy trial, witnesses and accusations.
Amendment VII: Right for a jury trial.

Amendment VIII: Bail and fines.
Amendment IX: Existence of other rights for the people
Amendment X: Power reserved to the states and people.

Later Amendments

Amendment XI: Suits against states.
Amendment XII: Election of executive branch.
Amendment XIII: Prohibition of slavery.
Amendment XIV: Privileges or immunities, due process, elections and debt: Consists of 5 sections and defines: (1) Citizenship (2) Apportionment of representatives among the states, (3) Rules for being a Senator or Representative, (4) Validity of the public debt, (5) Congressional Enforcement of this Article.
Amendment XV: Race and the right to vote.
Amendment XVI: Income tax.
Amendment XVII: Senator election and number.
Amendment XVIII: Prohibition on sale of alcohol
Amendment XIX: Gender and the right to vote.
Amendment XX: "Lame duck" session of Congress eliminated.
Amendment XXI: Repeal of Amendment XVIII (Prohibition).
Amendment XXII: Limit of Presidential terms.
Amendment XXIII: Election rules for the District of Columbia
Amendment XXIV: Taxes and the right to vote.
Amendment XXV: Rules of Presidential succession.
Amendment XXVI: Age and the right to vote.
Amendment XXVII: Pay raises and Congress

Amendments Never Ratified

Besides the above summary of the constitutional body of law, six other amendments have been proposed to the Constitution that have not been ratified and thus do not represent the law of the land. The entire text of these amendments is available freely on the Internet and in Brian Kelly's classic book in its third version, *Taxation Without Representation.*

What does this mean?

Here we are in a great book intended to help us all know how America was , is and will always be a great country. This chapter has given us a perspective on the government of the US and how it was created via the many patriotic documents discussed above. We now know that there were founding declarations and articles and we know about the many precepts in the Constitution as the primary law of the land.

Taxation was a major problem for the colonists and the representatives of the Second Congress, who, even during the war did not have taxing authority. There was never a welfare state in colonial or early America. Every buck that a colonist earned could theoretically be kept since the state's mission was not to provide for the welfare of others. The Constitution does not provide for redistribution of income.

Chapter 7 Are Americans Dumb Suckers?

Americans must stop being chumps

The fact that a doofus Governor of New York can be taken seriously when he suggests that America was never that great shows that something is wrong today in America. Our education system must be improved so we all know from whence America came, and why it is good and great.

Our representatives, such as Andrew Cuomo and his dad Mario Cuomo, are in office far too long. Not only can they make stupid proclamations with impunity, they gain illicit relationships with others in the ruling class and the donor class while they enjoy their multiple mini-reigns and the many perks to be had from their offices.

They begin to think that they belong in Washington DC, or the State Capitols, not their home territories, where their before-lives and their social-lives once existed. They begin to like the trappings of Washington etc. more than being with their loved ones back in their home cities and states. We can call that being corrupted in place.

From my vantage point as an observer, it is clear that Congress and many other offices at the state and federal level represents lobbyists, special interests and itself. Our representatives have no problem lying to our faces and working against us both publicly and privately. It seems easier for them to think of all Americans as chumps than to do their work on our behalf.

Unfortunately for all Americans, the new "important" relationships of public officials, especially our Congress, trump the notion of fair representation for the people (US) from back home. When they take their oaths of office and they promise to represent US, most are sincere at the time. But then…

Then, they come to Washington and experience the trappings and the temptations. And, because humans are only human, way too many of our finest stray from the mark and contribute to the re-creation of a country of which few thinking Americans are proud today.

Think about our forefathers, especially Thomas Jefferson who wrote the Declaration of Independence and of course George Washington, who guided our troops in the revolution against England's tyranny.

Think about honest Abe Lincoln, who freed the slaves and saved the union. These great patriots would weep to see what their political successors have done to our nation and to us individually. You can bet that in private and behind the gates of their communities, they mock us and have quite a laugh about what they pull off right before our eyes.

So, our fair-haired representatives (figure of speech) choose to represent themselves and their special interests, rather than the territories that sent them to the Congress of the USA to represent the people. Special interests provide special perquisites which overwhelm our greedy representatives and hold them in submission. Perhaps a dose of Lincoln's "honesty," is all that is needed to save the day. Wouldn't that be nice?

Our "honorable," do not even seem to care for our well-being. They care for their leadership positions, which make them big shots, and they care for themselves for sure. Unfortunately, they just can't get it into their heads that we the people are the reason they are employed in their official positions in the first place. By law, we are their employers, and they serve at our pleasure. The more we all understand that, the tighter the reins can be on reigning-in errant politicians, and the more the people will be in charge.

Then again, maybe a lot of the problem is our fault since we do not check them out well enough before we slam them into office. To make it simple to understand this notion—if there is a rotten piece of fish in the market and we select it for dinner, whose fault is it when it doesn't taste good and our guests get sick?

So, when we pick a rotten person to represent US—whose fault is that? You see, we do not have to be dummies about how all this happens. Too often, however, we choose to be. They don't get into a position to snooker us without us first electing them.

You and I have all heard our friends suggest that these knaves get into office because good men of position choose not to give of themselves. We all have said that it would be nice if a non-politician who is competent and honest were to run. It would be wonderful, right?

I regret to say that is a Utopia as the founders intended but even those who suggest they are looking for a non-politician, when in the voting booth are inclined to go with the politician rather than the person with "no experience." I know that from experience.

As I got older I thought I would give back so I know what I am talking about. I ran three times and made it to the ballot twice. Once was for Congress and once was for Mayor of my home town. The third time I let it be known I was willing to be a write-in. In both scenarios in which I made the ballot, my local paper endorsed entrenched politicians. I have a fine resume but in their rationale for endorsing the long-time politicians, they highlighted the fact that other than being President of the IBM Club in Scranton, PA, I had no political experience.

The irony of course is that all normal Americans want to put a person with no political experience and a lot of smarts into office. I thought that no political experience would be to my advantage. I now know that in the final analysis, the majority of the people vote with their stomachs and not with their brains.

I now have a theory that circulating experienced politicians out of office in short terms is the only solution to keeping them from controlling us. The people should permit only about five years in office and then no more. The best of us in my experience and in watching current events, do not want to vote in somebody who never held office. Yes, we certainly should -- all other things being equal. But, in my personal experience, we won't and don't.

The people get shortchanged

It does not matter whether the government is controlled by Democrats or Republicans. The people are always short-changed on the notion of representation and honesty! When has a representative run effectively on honesty? Is that because we do not care about honesty or we know they are kidding. Either way it is our fault.

We do get the government we deserve. It is time, however, that we begin to deserve better by paying attention and no longer voting with our stomachs. Voting with our stomachs makes us chumps of politicians who become our lords and masters.

Somebody once said that if you like your honesty, you will be able to keep it and it should save you about $2500.00 per year. But I jest, yet my jest is serious. You know the promise! It was Obama on healthcare.

OK, nobody said exactly that but some president at some time in the last eight years told Americans that they could keep their doctors, their health policies, and save $2500.00. A lot of chumps believed him and when it was found to be untrue, the same people could not wait to reelect him or his surrogate.

My objective in this book is not to have you know who said that or to get you upset whether he or she did or did not. I just want you to think about what the founders promised and what American government was delivering to the people before the liars took charge. If America was never great, and that is not true, then it would have been because our representatives failed US and we failed to stop them.

There is a chasm. Only your vote, the way the people swept Trump into office, can save the day. Now, we must help this still new President get rid of the bad guys—the Swamp, if you will or we are doomed.

And, so, from my own experience and research, my objective is to help smarten you up along with as many other Americans that I can reach and who will hear my message. The eight years before Trump taught us all that guys like that, whether they are the president or not, will treat you and I like chumps if we let them. And, so it is time to clean out the Congress and the Senate. For that of course, we cannot be voting in those with political experience. I know you get my drift.

I have the uncanny gift of being able to imitate other people's speech. In other words, I can impersonate certain people. In my home town, I can imitate the late Congressman, Daniel J. Flood, as if he were in the room with us. It is a gift. I can also imitate WC Fields, though not as well—but not too badly.

Can W. C. Fields help America today?

Some Americans know that WC Fields was the essence of Americana in his day. He found the nuances and he got a lot of laughs by pointing them out while using just a smidge of hyperbole. Fields counted on the weak and the strong alike to understand his missives, and he fired them off in his raspy voice to much acclaim.

Fields was into everybody's head, like it or not, strong willed-or not. He was not just a writer and an actor; he was also a psychologist without a degree. I would argue that only WC Fields can explain why America is falling apart today. However, I would agree to give Rod Serling his due. Today's battles between left and right may just be a bad Twilight Zone episode.

Fields did not think much of the human character of his day and age, and I suspect that he would think less of humans in our time. How about the title of one of his films? Does it not explain his perspective about how non-thinking humans, aka dummies and chumps, can be exploited when they choose to not pay attention?

I would ask you all to consider his movie, *"Never Give a Sucker an Even Break."* This is a war-time 1941 Universal Pictures comedy starring the raspy voiced master of comedy himself. WC wrote the original story without taking credit in his own name. His pseudonym for this work was Otis Criblecoblis. This master played himself in the movie. His plot was that he was searching for a chance to promote a surreal screenplay he had written. Ah, Yes!

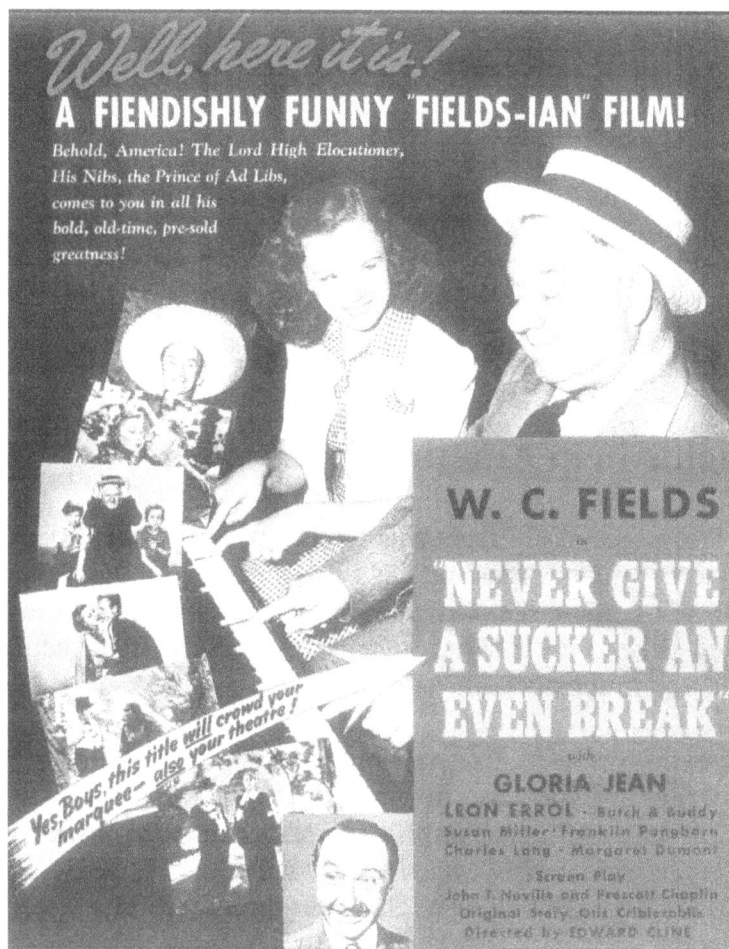

Fields based this movie on some of his earlier films, such as *Poppy* (1936) and *You Can't Cheat an Honest Man* (1939). It did not take long for the audience to know the poor regard Fields felt for his fellow man.

WC himself would refer to it as understanding the comic importance of human vulnerability. In *Poppy*, for example, he tells his sweet little daughter that "If we should ever separate, my little plum, I want to give you just one bit of fatherly advice: *"Never give a sucker an even break!"*

Think about that and ask yourself if you have wondered why some of the political parties out there today may not be giving any of US an even break. Maybe they think we are chumps, too weak to demand it?

Knowing that he had hit a chord with his Americana, in the blockbuster film, *You Can't Cheat an Honest Man*, WC lays it on even thicker. He knew that people hated wussies; but he also knew that many people take on the personality of a wuss, in a moment's notice.

And, so, in this great film extravaganza, with gin breath for sure in every scene, WC tells a customer that his grandfather's last words, "just before they sprung the trap" were, "You can't cheat an honest man; never give a sucker an even break, or smarten up a chump." He could say these seven thousand times in his inimitable voice, and I know I would chuckle each time. But, maybe he was right about US?

Since this is not supposed to be a heavy political book, though we are surely in tough political times, when trust of government is in question, I cannot tell you which of the two major political parties think that Americans have no brains. It seems that the opinion is shared by both. However, I will tell you that WC Fields would have had no problem identifying the culprits and delivering the goods.

Moreover, he would have been pleased to cheat suckers in any way he could; while giving none a break. All chumps of course would remain dumb and gullible and capable of swallowing political propaganda, while still remaining loyal to the Party that was inflicting the most harm on them. Does that sound like today's Democrats? Fields in many ways behaved as the Party. He lied very well. In fact, he literally made prevarication into an art form.

My job in this book is to help all Americans know that it is about time that we all pay attention and that we no longer defer to the judgment of political "friends." Let's stop being suckers and chumps, and throw out the bums that are destroying America, from whichever party they come. Don't let them say America was never great!

If we happen to come across an upstanding janitor in a clean building, we would be far better off enticing this fine person into representing our district than listening to the propaganda of the establishment political class. They are destroying America. Their advice is purposely directed to convince US to elect representatives of the worst character. Let's just say no!

When Fields put out his last film, he was 61 years old. Though he was probably tickled that he lasted to 62 years of age, with all the weathering he inflicted on himself over the years, he knew that alcohol and illness had taken their toll. His waist line had grown in size but not by design. He loved a nip way too much. It would do him in and soon.

He was an accomplished juggler in his teens and early days in burlesque. He had real athletic talent, and he had the determination of a poor person, hoping never again to be poor.

At one time, when in his fifties, he went through a period in which he made eight films in the space of two years. Abuse does take its toll. I bring him into this book because Americans are being played for chumps by the political class, and nobody seems to be giving US a break.

Truth and knowledge are our best hope to fight off the promises and lies of the political class such as Andrew Cuomo. Don't let anybody damn America—even the infamous entrenched Swamp. When you see a politician speaking, remember there is only one way to know if he or she is lying: "Are his lips moving?"

Then, of course in today's day and age, you have the low-information voters – the most gullible citizens, who are so good hearted, they would ask an aggressor if they could hold the nail as the aggressor pounded it through their hands on a cross.

They would ask an opposing soccer striker coming towards the ball in a rush to kick it into the goal, "Is this your ball sir?" They would be nice rather than take what is theirs. They would not want the striker to miss out on her or his opportunity to score. Why kick it away to save the team when there is less immediate flack if you just say, "Oh, excuse me, is this your ball?"

That's just a little too nice for real Americans. But that is where participation trophies take young to-be millennial athletes. Why get better? Why get wise? America was not born of niceness. It was built on fairness, goodness, and individual strength.

We the people are not supposed to give politicians an even break; we are supposed to pay attention so our rights are not violated by grabby, greedy politicians. If you happen to be in this low information / overly nice category, thank you for visiting this book. I hope that through my writings, I can help you be more like you can be.

You gotta smarten up or we are all toast. Finish this book, please and I hope that you will understand how smart you can be and how much power you can wield against those who care nothing about you or me, or America. Always keep your eye on the ball and do not give the ball up to an opponent just because they lie and schmooze you.

Though I enjoy his work, please note that this is not a biography of WC Fields nor is it a book that attempts to hide all of his transgressions or the transgressions of the political class. Beware of false prophets.

Fields was the master in understanding his times. My goal in bringing him into this discussion as we absorb this book, is so that we can cast his knowledge forward to the people of today and we can all gain. With a not-so-free and very dishonest and corrupt press, spewing more fake news than news, the propaganda provided by the mainstream media of today, would have US all believe in the *"Tooth Fairy."* Any of US that live by believing the rot of the Swamp entrenched media, are un-smartened chumps.

Since I too believe in Santa Clause, and have met him once or twice in my life, I will cast aspersions only on the Tooth Fairy. I have never personally met her, though I did find a quarter under my pillow one morning where once a missing tooth had been placed. But, the quarter from my jeans pocket was unexplainably missing. And, so, one of my very own guiding principles is: "There is no free lunch!"

Ask the mainstream press about these two fine characters, which make our children very happy. Ask them if they are real or not? If you can get the press to talk to you honestly about Santa or the Tooth Fairy, ask them if they care at all about regular Americans.

Those of US living in the shadow of the post 2008 and 2012 elections are no longer suffering from a recession or a bad economy. Sorry, just kidding! We all have been told that we are in a recovery period by a government that would say anything to protect its power.

How did this recovery go for you? Were you OK? For me Trump promised relief and the deep state is blocking the full measure of the relief our new president could be delivering. We must rid ourselves of the political swamp by not being chumps. Send the rogues packing.

You and I both know that for eight whole years we had been suffering from no economy if not worse than that. The lack of any prosperity was caused by a government that wanted to punish anybody or any company that was productive. Those in charge of government pre-Trump told us all that this was the new normal and we were just supposed to accept less. They also said it would never get better.

The man who promised hope and change made it so that eventually the people hoped that the changes to come would not hurt as much as the changes that had come. If we think those eight years were bad, can you imagine no countervailing power. Can you imagine if, God forbid, in the future they are able to depose or impeach our duly elected President with the help of a crooked court system and they paste in a Hillary or a Hillary-like stooge to pretend he or she is the new Obama. Perhaps like Hollywood stars, we would be able to move out of the country to a nice place—where all the following famous people said they would go:

1. Jon Stewart
Still in USA.
2. Chelsea Handler
Still in USA.
3. Neve Campbell
Still in USA.
4. Barry Diller
Still in USA.
5. Lena Dunham
Still in USA.
6. Keegan-Michael Key
Still in USA.
7. Chloë Sevigny
Still in USA.
8. Al Sharpton

Still in USA.
9.Natasha Lyonne
Still in USA.
10. Eddie Griffin
Still in USA.
11. Spike Lee
Still in USA.
12. Amber Rose
Still in USA.
13. Samuel L Jackson
Still in USA.
14. Cher
Still in USA.
15. George Lopez
Still in USA.
16. Barbra Streisand
Still in USA.
17. Raven-Symonè
Still in USA.
18. Whoopi Goldberg
Still in USA.
19. Omari Hardwick
Still in USA.
20. Miley Cyrus
Still in USA.
21. Ruth Bader Ginsburg
Still in USA.
22. Amy Schumer
Still in USA.
23. Katie Hopkins
Still in USA.

Whoops! Looks like we are already there!

I did not accept it then and I hope you won't ever accept it. This was about the worst governing period that I had ever lived through. But, because we still had the right to vote, you and I helped put in Donald Trump. I ask you to always vote when you feel outraged but maybe if you vote each time—even before you are outraged, we can cut the bad years and the bad representatives off at the pass.

The Affordable Health Care Act, which cynics either call the Unaffordable Health Care Act, or simply Obamacare (even the past President loves the term), is one of those things that most Americans joke about in public but fear in private. Most of US get sick every now and then and we do not want a government bureaucrat deciding whether we get treatment or not.

We may joke about its conception and its most inept rollout, and the miracle of a 7.1 million subscriber count four years later by March 31, 2014—when just the day before nobody knew how many had paid. These things are really not funny, but our government presents the truth as its mortal enemy.

How
Obamacare
REALLY works

The Insurance Industry | State Gov't | Obama

YOU | Don't you feel healthier already?

www.publiusforum.com

We were all suckers and chumps to have accepted Obamacare and to reelect legislators who would not get rid of it. Some of the most attractive measures of Obamacare included the fact that it permitted parents to keep their kids on the healthcare dole until they were 26 years of age.

Ironically, since the Obama economy was so bad, even college graduates could not get jobs and so they could not get healthcare. Therefore, they needed their parents plans as a crutch. I used it myself and learned that though my daughter got health insurance, I had a hard time affording it. The other great thing people like is that nobody can deny a person enrollment even if they have a pre-existing condition.

Well, I have bad news about the lies in this story. Just like you can't keep your doctor, your hospital, or your health insurance plan, and you will never see $2500 in savings, despite Obama promises, he was also kidding about pre-existing conditions. Obama said, you can get Obamacare if you have a pre-existing condition. Sorry, he was kidding again. Please forgive him as you always do simply because he was once president.

Let's pick a point in time such as March 31, 2014. That was the first real Obamacare deadline. It was the last day to take advantage of open enrollment and if you did not enroll, there would be no coverage for preexisting conditions and the age 26 child inclusion was null and void also.

So, back then and every year since, unless you could postpone your illness until January of 2015, or 2016, or 2017, or 2018, etc., and you did not die beforehand, you were not permitted to sign up for Obamacare—including the preexisting condition option. At this time, there were just 7.1 million signed up out of 330,000,000 Americans. With the then President claiming a big victory at the time, nobody in 2014 could get insurance again until 2015. Who did that help?

I know that the prior President did not tell anybody that, but it is the truth. No bad news about the results from liberal leadership is ever disseminated by a corrupt press.

The government had no problem not providing what it had promised. They simply informed the people before the deadline as if it were not Obama's fault: *"the clock is ticking on the individual health insurance open enrollment period for 2014, which is scheduled to end on March 31, 2014."* When the clock ran out, that was it – no coverage for anything until a year later—even though there were just over 7 million of 325 million covered.

Moreover, unlike many of the other deadlines established under "Obamacare," this one would not be extended or delayed and it was not. Health and Human Services Secretary Kathleen Sebelius told Congress on March 12, 2014 that the Obama administration would not extend the deadline for people to sign up for health insurance or delay the requirement for most Americans to have coverage. That was that but many have already forgotten that act of severe callousness. What were people without coverage to do?

What did this mean and what has it meant every year hence? It means that, if you had not already done so, you had only until the end of March of that year to obtain minimally adequate coverage for yourself and your dependents, either through your state health insurance exchange, directly from a private health insurer, or anywhere else you could find it. Even the online system did not work. I think we have already had enough of Obamacare. You?

Regardless of which Party is responsible for the mess, Americans have been played for chumps, sitting on the edge, anticipating that somehow, because there are big problems, we would all get nailed by Obamacare in one way or another

Are Americans of today suckers & chumps?

.

Chapter 8 Spurn Corrupt Politicians and Be an American Patriot

America is a great country! I think an American can do anything if they are inspired! Watch out for the crooks in government.

Hard work pays off big time?

America has always been a capitalist country in which hard work pays off big-time, and so the same goes for our economy. If any American political party comes-by led by Democrats or Republicans, and it wants to change America into a communist, socialist, or Marxist country, once you understand America, and you are no longer part of the low-information crowd, you will be well-equipped with the information you are absorbing to fire off a resounding "NO" in our native language of English.

As a proud American, after I wrapped up most of my IT career, I thought that I might be able to help my country with the knowledge and skills that I had picked up as an American citizen, who happened to be a well-trained and well experienced IT professional.

I was "baptized" at King's College with a Data Processing degree and later I was baptized by fire in technical and marketing skills by the IBM Corporation itself. At the time, IBM was king of all IT in the world. Then later I received MBA status at Wilkes University because I wanted to know more about business.

So, here I am in early post retirement. I stopped actively seeking IT engagements for my consulting practice, though I get some anyway, and I am actually thinking about reemerging in IT sometime in the near future. Maybe!

But, while my resources were more abundant, and I saw an America failing and becoming as poorly managed as a banana republic, I began to re-study my American heritage, with an eye to doing my part to keep our country strong.

I hoped to learn how to keep America beyond the reach and influence of treacherous politicians, who would be pleased with tyranny, simply to gain an extra nickel for their over-bulging pocket books and wallets.

That led me into making a run for the US Congress without taking a dime from relatives or friends, or anybody else. I learned many lessons from this great attempt. Unfortunately, my biggest lesson was that when a regular citizen chooses to run for national office, the bumps in the road to possible success are huge. They are not just little moguls that can be quickly overcome.

The game is rigged against regular Americans by guess-who—corrupt politicians from the last 150 years. We are chumps to them. They are not about to give up their power easily, even if we the people demand it. President Trump has learned this lesson in trying to clean out a swamp of corruption while the swamp itself does not want to be cleansed. Our only recourse is to vote them out, while elections in the US are still permitted and still free, and the workers in the crooked election stations may still be prosecuted if they mess with us.

Supposed representatives of the people from years past have placed obstacle after obstacle in the path of any non-political potential candidates. Their objective is for US to learn our lessons and never attempt to disrupt the harmony that all crooked politicians have among themselves.

Many of the founders engaged George III of England so America could be free without a revolution. Those from countries other than England who came to America engaged other Kings and royalty in addition to King George III. But, all came to America to be free. I hope all Americans wake up to realize that freedom is not free.

The founders never envisioned that tyranny would come from the people itself and from the press. They never expected the citizenry to stand by and permit the powerful to take away the liberties for which the revolutionaries shed blood. Our founders would not be happy with many of US today, because we sit idly by like chumps and let things happen to US.

They said no to the repression of freedom and took matters into their own hands, risking life and limb, to provide US with a free America, in which all of the people are free. Go get yourself a breath of fresh air. It is free. It is brought to you by the founders.

Unfortunately, because of neglect from our representatives, a whole new bunch of people arrived inside our country without checking in. They did not come because we are free in America, they came because they could take things from us for free. They can even take American jobs with the tacit acceptance of the American government. If they could not get a job, their sustenance would also be free from our welfare system paid by John Q. Public. How nice are we while we are starving, to give others our food?

Today, the well-to-do politicians, who have become very popular with the low-information Americans, along with sharp and cunning regular folks with political ambitions, are happy to say or do anything that would help them get elected to important offices within the city, the state or elsewhere within the union.

The word "politician," is used in its most un-complimentary way to describe those who gain the people's trust and get elected to office and then turn on the people for their own self-interests.

The founders were well aware of politicians in England and other countries in Europe, and the treachery they caused. Back in the late 1700's as the Constitution was prepared for ratification, the founders were so tickled that George III was no longer in control, they somehow felt that the new America would remain pure over time and would not require another popular revolution to purify the government of scoundrels who may in later years choose to take control. Though their work was excellent, scoundrels still flourish.

The founders could not conceive of a scenario in which the recently freed American people would join an oppressive and tyrannical government, such as ours is today. Where we are today, it assures that the worst of the worst get to decide which freedoms and liberties the people should be left with.

The founders had created a set of rules, known as The Constitution to assure that all the people would be left with all freedom and all liberty in all cases. They did not want any scoundrels (politicians) messing with this notion or this nation.

Unfortunately, our legislators and our past president have stopped full adherence to the Constitution and consequently, our freedom is now in jeopardy. Our new President promises a return to greatness and so we will see if he can get that done with the deep state and the swamp fully engaged. Our representatives can stop this tonight or tomorrow; but, last time I checked, they are more interested in being important in Washington than helping the folks back home.

Only Americans who hope to be in control of a socialist state advocate against the American way. Egalitarian principles of socialism simply mean that nobody gets to be the cream of the crop since the most equal spot for all is the bottom of the barrel.

Before this is fait accompli, Americans who love freedom have to do a little more than just speak up. We have to know what the founders would do to protect liberty and freedom and we simply have to do it or suffer the consequences. Reading this book is a good start.

I do not have to preach freedom to 99% of Americans out there. We all either are products of good people who came here to be free or we came here ourselves to be free.

Permitting politicians from either party to talk us out of our birthright is not only dumb; it is asinine.

Yet, we can choose to be the dumbest Americans of all time. We can be chumps worthy of no respect if we choose. Or we can decide to engage, smarten up, stop acting dumb, and we can take on these bad guys. We cannot let them win. They do not care at all about us. Think of the leaders of the regimes that committed the atrocities that prompted our forefathers or ourselves to come to America. They were evil. They were bad. They would love to have their boot on your neck right now if you would let them.

I have had the pleasure of writing a lot of patriotic books. I write tech books and patriotic / political books. This is # 126. It is really fun to write these books and to help people with clear thinking.

Sometimes I do get the idea that I am talking to the wall. But, I am committed to do my part to help save America. Thank you for doing your part.

Each time I write a book, I hope that I can attract another person into a love affair with America. If you have read any of my other stuff, you know that I point out the bad guys and I pull no punches in my description of what we must do to escape from their reach. They will destroy us if we do not pay attention.

In one of my books titled *The Federalist Papers, by Hamilton, Jay, and Madison*, I wrote no more than twenty pages of original introductory text to help persuade the reader that the rest of the book for which they had paid was worth reading. I admit I did more than that.

I took the patriotic essays of Alexander Hamilton, John Jay, and James Madison, known as The Federalist Papers, and I separated all of the two page and single page paragraphs, and half page paragraphs, and other large paragraphs, and I chopped them into smaller, more readable bits and pieces. Whether you buy The Federalist Papers by Brian W. Kelly or you download these essays free of charge, there is a lot of learning to be had about the formation of our government and how it is supposed to work in the Federalist Papers.

I literally had to wake myself up too many times in my initial reading because the Federalist Papers are tough to read but well worth the read. They are very insightful. I know how tough it is to get through them as written because I read each and every essay from start to finish in original form before I put them in more readable form in my book. I did not eliminate a word of the original. I just made them all more readable. Check them out at https://www.amazon.com/Federalist-Papers-Hamilton-Jay-Madison/dp/0989995739.

By the way, just like *America 4 Dummmies*, another book that I wrote years ago, this patriotic book cites the US Constitution, The Declaration of Independence, The Articles of Confederation, The Bill of Rights, and lots of other stuff that many of US over the years have forgotten. You can read them all on the Internet. I included them in America 4 Dummmies but it did make the book more expensive and that is why I did not add the 100 pages to this book.

Once you get back into the great writings of the founders, you will fully understand that they are the glue that keeps Americans free and they can help provide US all with liberty and justice forever and ever and ever… as long as we pay attention.

Having read the Federalist Papers myself, I feel like I should not be the one to offer this exhortation, but I shall anyway. If you can read every one of the Federalist Papers, you have passed a great love test for America, and if you do all the other things you need to do to be the citizen you would be proud to be, you then become worthy of the title, American. I love having that title.

Those of US who read the Federalist Papers, though it is an arduous journey, know we have accomplished a lot. These papers—eighty- five articles written by Alexander Hamilton, John Jay, and James Madison, quickly show US all that the founders were very concerned that the bad aspects of any other foreign government would not become part of the new American Democratic Republic.

The founders were well aware of politicians, but since they never put the notion of welfare, food stamps, and cell phones in the founding documents, they did not believe that the people would permit the Republic to be tainted by notions like socialism, progressivism, or Marxism.

In the early days, the people were all aware of the blood sacrifices the early colonials had made to secure the new America. Never in the history of man was so much patriotism shown for a notion that might not ever make it to the future. After enduring tyranny from England and other monarchies, Americans fought for and won the revolution against England et al for the cause of liberty and freedom.

Yet, here we were 200 plus years later in 2008, looking for hope and change rather than looking to the spirits of our founders to rebuild our fallen nation. We elected a president for eight years. This President did Americans few favors and even today, from what I see, he operates in the Deep State to help undermine the current president. What a shame! Hope will deliver nothing when action by well spirited citizens is required but discouraged.

So, again, why did I write this book?

I have found so many people, including myself, who at one time have forgotten the sacrifices of the revolutionaries and the gifts of freedom and liberty that were bestowed on all of US at the time of the revolutionary war victory and the subsequent formation of our governing document, namely, The Constitution.

Andrew Cuomo and a bunch of millennials need to reread the founding document s so they know the greatness of the founding of our country.

We Americans have been so blessed that we have not reminded ourselves enough over the years of our great heritage. Fourth of July celebrations are much more than picnics, and though our parents tried for us to understand, the work of our founders is often lost in the celebration.

Yet, neither freedom nor liberty come cheap so the next time an engaging politician offers you something for nothing, and in your heart, you know it is wrong; stick to your guns. Remember the words of Ben Franklin, a favorite US and Pennsylvania patriot:

"Those who desire to give up freedom in order to gain security will not have, nor do they deserve, either one."

Chapter 9 Have Democrats and the Corrupt Press Gone Nuts?

Is Trump responsible for all the bad in the world?

After trying to subtly impeach President Trump for being ill-suited for office from the moment he was sworn in on January 20, 2017, the left has simply gone nuts. Nothing is worse of course than when on Thursday August 17, Democratic Senator Maria Chappelle-Nadal said: "I hope Trump is assassinated. The left-driven corrupt press and the Democratic Party itself seems to have developed a collective brain disease as their actions and desires are beyond reason.

Andrew Cuomo and his millennial followers may have misspoken but even they are not as bad as those just a few more feet to the left.

They are insane. Everything that President Trump does is suspect according to these nut-bags. They'll have you believe that it was from the moment of his "dark" inauguration speech in which he vowed to transfer power from political elites back to the people that he was out of touch with reality. Yet, none of them try to explain why there is something wrong with the people regaining the power.

And, of course, with eight months of continual Russia, Russia, Russia, in between, the media theme first changed to Trump's insensitivity to slavery and his natural racial bias. Now it is former idiots from the Obama Regime coming out and saying the President Trump is not fir for office. Unfortunately for Americans the press first prints their lies then they read them and then they cite them as fact.

The fact is that I never voted for President Obama. But, I took him as my president for sure. I did not like most of what he did as I felt it undermined the country, but I did not say he was a nut job or needed to be impeached. When I saw an Obama, T-shirt being worn or a bumper sticker, I let it pass. He was the president. Not so with the left. It is getting bad out there as cars with Trump bumper stickers are getting keyed and those wearing a Trump hat or a Trump T-shirt etc. are being attacked on the street. That surely cannot help America. Trump is our president.

The leftist leadership and the corrupt press recently suggested that by President Trump's admonition in the Charlottesville riots that both sides are at fault and his insistence that it takes two to tango, he is a racist and his speech is a racist. Whew! Yet this makes no sense and it is out of line with the truth. The truth of course is the truth and it stands by itself--unaltered by the insane rhetoric and mindless pressure from the left.

Who can deny that a classic clash of the far left with the far right has antagonist and protagonist elements. But, upon reflection, we know we would be declared wrong by the biased press. Was this event, which was planned by permit months earlier by the right, just too much to pass up by those on the left wanting to make a statement without getting a permit?

Was it incited by the wind or by two groups possessing dissimilar thought patterns? Even Democrats are now seeing that the only real dark messages in these troubled times are coming from the darkness and extreme hate of the left. Why hate so much?

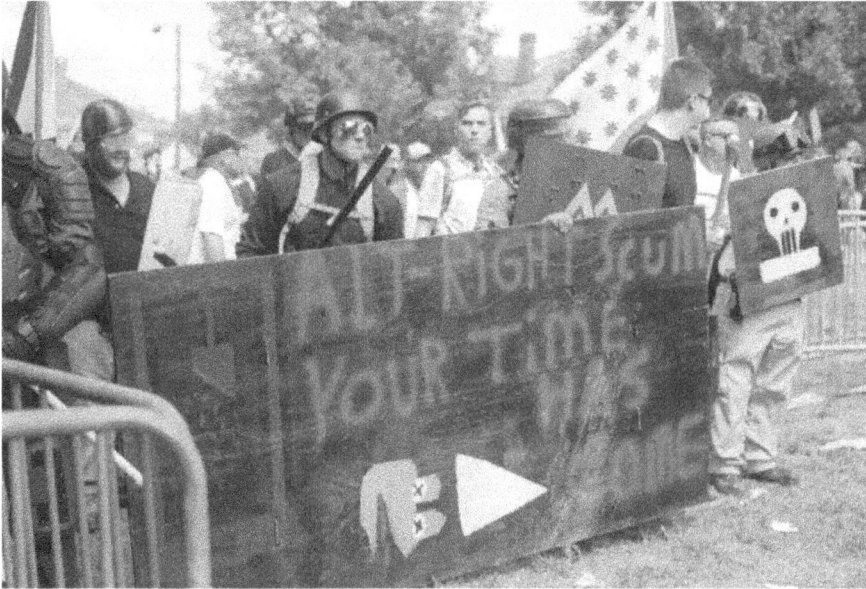

The press, of course who are 99 44/100% anti-Trump and anti-conservative took sides and blamed those with a permit and not those who crashed the party and brought in clubs and weapons to meet what was supposed to be a peaceful protest enabled by a lawful permit. This event was not a rally of Trump supporters. Looking at the last few years, we know that Trump supporters for the most part do not have violent tendencies and they also have poor regard for white supremacists?

Clearly Trump supporters in the main are regular people, not part of a KKK or neo Nazi movement. In fact, there may be only 20,000 KKK members in the country. Trump supporters would not let one of this crowd in any meeting.

Many blacks are part of the Trump support group but the corrupt press will not tell you that. I serve with them as Trump and I are both color-blind. You might know that Trump and his supporters do not support the extreme right agenda of the far-right groups nor do they support the extreme left agenda of far left-groups.

But you would not know that based on some of the reporting flying around in Charlottesville week. If there were no leftists determined to mess up the day, the day could have been peaceful. For some it would have been disgusting but it still would have been peaceful.

There is no question that it was some white nationalists who got a permit, defended it in court, and went ahead and staged a march in Charlottesville Virginia over the removal of Confederate statues. That is their right. The white nationalists followed the law in that they asked for and received a permit for their rally.

The City later moved their rally from where they wanted it to another location. They went to court and the ACLU obtained an order granting their rally at the original location. The ACLU is normally not against leftist causes. The left however, had not received a permit for their action intended to disrupt the far-right rally.

So, the facts of the incident show that a throwback Antifa crowd from the 1930's and 1940's decided to show up at the rally and the results were what any sane person would have predicted. There was violence. One woman, Heather Heyer, was killed and a number of other people were injured. Without Antifa, there would have been no major commotion though the nut job with the van may still have done his dirt. Antifa has recently been the subject of a poll that looks to label them as a terrorist organization. We'll see what happens on that one.

Antifa, is a far-left wing fascist group, whose name ironically stands for "Anti-fascist." Someone called Antifa "a bunch of washed up losers, living in their parents' basement." Others suggest that is not an accurate picture since it looks like a few of them wash very often. That gives a perspective that there is no love lost between the KKK and Black Lives Matter but we knew that already. Why they go to each other's rallies is what creates the violence.

The white Nationalists see Democrats as trying to redefine their role in the Civil War – the role of slaveholders. It was not conservatives or Republicans who were anti-black and pro-slavery. It was and in many places, still is the Democratic Party. Ask yourself why did the traditionally pro-slavery Democrats suddenly decide that the time had come for the demolition of the monument to General Lee, the

Commander of the Democrat South Army? The commander-in-chief, who was against slavery?

This monument stood in a park in the center of historical Charlottesville for about 100 years. It was a quiet park not deserving of much attention. Along with pigeons, doves and other birds, people walked peacefully in this park. Old men played chess as a ritual. The statue to some was a reminder that in the Civil War, the Southern Democrats lost to the Republican Northerners. The monument was erected by Democrats, not Republicans even though their general Robert E. Lee, adorned in the statue was a staunch anti-slavery advocate who was fighting for states' rights, not man's inhumanity to man. Ironically, he was fighting against Democrats.

It was the Republicans who came along when Lincoln was president. They took the slaves from their democratic masters over the objection of Democratic leadership. Ironically, the Democrats who constructed the Civil War monuments to commemorate their brave dead, decided to trash their own monuments.

A recent poll shows a majority of Americans (62%) want to keep Confederate statues in place to "honor" fallen leaders of the South. Less than a majority of today's Democrats (47%) want the statue defacing and removal to continue.

A who's who of the protesters in Charlottesville speaks for itself. The backbone of the protest is the Ku Klux Klan, who the Southern Poverty Law Center cite as numbering between 5000 and 8,000 and no more than 20,000 in total. The corrupt press of course wants to give the idea that there are millions of nasty white people who are either in the Klan or favor its activities. We can call that "fake news." Or lies whichever your pleasure.

There is no question that the it is now politically correct to call anybody with a sentiment to the Klan as, "White Supremacists" Those who understand history recognize the Ku Klux Klan as a racist organization created by Democrats after the Civil War to control the black population. Most blacks and many regular Democrats have forgotten the role of the Democrats in the slave trade and the continual desire to subjugate the black population. The corrupt press of course blames

Republicans for slavery and thus they are the promulgators of lies and fake news.

These guys who blame Republicans for everything perfectly remember their origins, but they can't admit it. Nonetheless it was the Klan, a pro-Democrat, pro-left group, who held the major nighttime torchlight procession on the eve of street fighting in Charlottesville. One of the former leaders of the Ku Klux Klan, the infamous David Duke (who, incidentally, only six months ago publicly supported the candidacy of anti-Semite Keith Ellison for the post of chairman of the Democratic Party of the United States) was one of the participants at the rally.

In Charlottesville, a group known as neo-Nazis were also widely represented. These guys are a typical product of the American educational system. They do not seem to understand that Nazism is a kind of socialism, as advocated by Democrats, not Republicans. Socialism of course is, an extremely leftist, not a right-sided ideology. From the program of the National Socialist Workers Party of Germany (this notorious program was written personally by Hitler and consists of 25 points) they forget all the points except one – racism, because the faux news corrupt media can make a lot of hay labeling and blaming Republicans as the racists while knowing that racism has been part of the platform of the Democratic since the days of slavery in the US.

Nonetheless, these modern followers of the fascist swastika do not know anything about this history. Therefore, they are like babes, showing no resistance to the fact that well-educated leftists call them "right-wingers." Political correctness in many ways is incongruous to rational thought. Inscrutable are your ways, political correctness.

We have learned that These two groups, the Klan and the Neo Nazis, both with strong Democratic pro-slavery leanings while in Charlottesville, were opposed by bandit formations of Antifa. The litany of Antifa subgroups include Black Lives Matter (BLM), American Communists, and Democratic Socialists of America (DSA).

Of course, it would take just a small amount of research and a real search for the truth, for a casual observer to recognize that The Nazi origins of the "antifascist" movement of Antifa, sponsored by the Nazi accomplice George Soros, has long been known. BLM is a black racist terrorist organization sponsored by the same Soros.

The DSA is famous for the fact that it was young Barack Obama who joined the party as soon as he arrived in Chicago. DSA is a member of the Socialist International. Who is kidding whom? Yet, on the nightly fake news, you would never get the truth in a million years. Democratic leaders cannot afford for their supporters to know the truth about their long-term relationship with slavery and black oppression.

Photo: Democratic Party Convention. New York, 1924

If the mainstream fake news press were to show this photo, they would be forced to tell one of their whopper lies and say that it was Republicans marching. Dear Democrats, your party and your press have been lying for quite a while. What's a few more lies about Trump?

If you are a regular American and you went to Charlottesville to protest the pulling down of General Lee's statue, more than likely, though your cause was acceptable to most, you more than likely would have left the gathering. The normally disgusting methods deployed by both groups of nasty people were not hidden from the masses. Both sides of the conflict appeared in Charlottesville with a full parade – with flags (swastika, hammer and sickle prevailing). Banners, feces, urine, pepper spray bottles, batons, clubs and other riot gear were readily available and were in full use.

What can regular people do about the statue epidemic?

Though for the past year, the statue epidemic has quieted down, when the leftist run out of material, we can expect them to bring it back like an old Perry Mason re-run.

One thing for sure in this debate. The left is not interested in any debate. Though as we point out in this book, the left were the major slave masters with Democrats fighting the abolition of slavery tooth and nail from the beginning of the country.

No argument however, appeases the left's thirst to rip down memorials that the left itself put up in their support of slavery. You see, it is not about slavery. It is about their perception that America is illegitimate and that it must become a socialist or communist state to be OK with itself. Most Americans do not want that.

So, a broader leftist agenda is at work here. The first objective is to label a huge number of common symbols racist. The movement to tear down statues is moving along so that Thomas Jefferson is being targeted now as he once owned slaves. They want to stop students from wearing the American flag to school on Cinco De Mayo. They want to have everybody become Colin Kaepernick by completely ending the playing of the National Anthem at football games.

The Confederate flag and the Confederate war memorials are only their first step toward that goal. It's rather obvious that the Left has no such interest in tearing down statues of Robert Byrd in the U.S. Capitol or Vladimir Lenin in Seattle. Why is that. It is because the whole thing is a ruse for a major change in the US government.

Another major objective is to tear down any symbols they want without due process of law. Law gets in the way of the left's goal of anarchy on the way to a new order of socialism and communism for America. You can see that in Durham. You can see it in the vandalism directed against statues elsewhere. It is the left's broad-based plan to legitimize lawbreaking and violence. The legitimization of anti-lawful activities with police standing down has led to the growth of movements like Antifa, which spreads violence in its wake.

Nobody said racism is not a problem. It is a bigger problem today because of eight years of Obama who pledged to end it. Racism, regardless of the kick start it got by Obama having police stand down during riots is a big problem, and it must be fought. But the bigger problem is that racism cannot be fought while the far left and the far right are clubbing each other over the head and destroying each other's property.

In fact, the leading growth-point for the alt-right is leftist violence and overreach. The right is being stimulated to act in many ways to protest the left's lawlessness. If the Left truly wished to defeat racism, they would need to start by ending both their violence and their pathetic attempts to label anyone who disagrees with their policy prescriptions racist. Ben Shapiro says it well: "Breaking leftist toes on metal statues of long-dead Confederate soldiers isn't solid strategy, and it isn't good for the country."

Meanwhile the American public feels officials are not stopping the vandalism and violence, and this has the potential to lead to all-out violence from two clashing ideologies. Once a statue is gone, it is gone forever. Why? When the statue does not really matter at all. These are public monuments and if the public wants them destroyed fine but if not, this is a dangerous formula and sooner than later, Americans with firearms are going to get into the act. Lawlessness brings vigilantism.

In Houston, for example, the idea of shooting statue vandals in the act is being discussed as I write. The question being debated is not whether statue desecration is OK it is "Does Texas law allow you to shoot a protester if you see him or her defacing a Confederate statue?" This is very dangerous. The problem can get lots worse before it gets better especially as Mayors and Governors allow this lawlessness to go on with impunity.

A Texas man, for example, claiming to be a police academy instructor says the answer is yes. We're verifying this troubling claim that's gone viral. Phil Ryan made the post on Facebook. He cites all sorts of criminal statutes in Texas and ends by writing "Bottom line, if someone is destroying a monument or statue that isn't theirs, you can defend it by force during the day, with deadly force at night." The question in Texas thus is "should people begin to shoot the vandals?" So far, I have not heard no good ideas for how officials plan to stop this or at least call a moratorium. Why would the left stop when they are having it their way by not debating?

Charlottesville is not the only ruse

Even before Charlottesville, as the left was transitioning a bit from Russia, Russia, Russia, having chosen not to do the people's business this time around in Congress, they were searching for more bone-crushing fake news against President Trump.

It was just in May 2017, that Democratic Senator Ed Markey delivered what seemed like an explosive bit of news during an interview with CNN: A grand jury had been impaneled in New York, he said, to investigate the Trump campaign's alleged collusion with Russia. "Wow!" Said the left: "Great news!"

There was just one and only problem: It wasn't true.

The precise origins of the rumor have been difficult to pin down; but its tracings had been ricocheting around social media for days before Markey's interview. The story had no reliable sourcing, and not a single credible news outlet touched it—but it had been fervently championed by The Palmer Report, a progressive blog known for peddling conspiracy theories, and by anti-Trump Twitter crusaders like Louise Mensch. It was fake news at its worst.

Soon enough, prominent people with blue checkmarks by their names were amplifying it with "Big if true"-type Tweets. And by May 11, the story had migrated from the bowels of the internet to the mouth of a United States Senator.

After Markey's office apologized for spreading the unsubstantiated story, there was a mild flurry of articles warning of "fake news" aimed at the left, and then everyone moved on. But the episode jarringly illustrated an under-examined phenomenon in American politics.

Over the past two decades, an immense amount of left-leaning journalistic energy was spent exploring the right-wing media ecosystem—from talk radio, to Fox News, to Breitbart and beyond—and documenting its growing influence on mainstream GOP politics. This turned out to be a worthy and judicious pursuit, and if any doubt remains about that, it helps to recall that Donald J. Trump became the President.

While serious Republicans in the political class spent years scoffing at the "entertainers," such as Reagan, and "provocateurs" on the supposedly powerless fringe, the denizens of the fever swamp were busy taking over the party.

Now, here we sit in 2017 and some are asking: "Could the same thing happen on the left?"

Wayne Allen Root, an Obama classmate at Columbia.

On Wayne Allen Root's Facebook page, he has had a little fun with a recent rant that he made that got a lot of press. It is designed to make us think. The title of his diatribe is "Liberal Nutcases' Are Driving America Toward Civil War." On his Facebook page Root sums up an article written by Kyle Mantyla on June 27, 2017. Root says:

"Exactly. I couldn't have said it better myself. Oops, actually I did say it!." http://rootforamerica.com/

Wayne Allen Root is a patriot for sure. 1

Here is what Mantyla wrote:

"Right-wing commentator, conspiracy theorist and Donald Trump–obsessed sycophant Wayne Allyn Root unleashed a rant on his radio program last Friday, warning that America is headed for a civil war because the state of California is banning non-essential state travel to a handful of states that have enacted laws allowing discrimination against LGBTQ people.

"Are we headed for civil war?" Root asked. "I feel like it's 1860 again and we're in the months before a civil war in the United States of America."

"Can you imagine how sick these people are?" he continued. "You can't ban a Muslim from America who comes from a country that hates America and is rife with terrorism and they kill people left and right for being Christians, Jews or Americans and you don't want to let them in the country because you want your children to be safe and that's no good? But, God forbid, you ban transgender bathrooms, California say no one can travel there anymore ... So it's okay to ban American states because they don't like transgender people who are confused whether they have a penis or a vagina?"

"This is so stupid that it defies description, but it's also a sign of mental illness," Root ranted. "Liberals are mentally ill ... We're out of our minds and we're headed for civil war, it's pretty clear."

"These people are crazy," he said. "They want a war. They don't like you and me, they want to hurt us or kills us! These people are absolutely nuts ... Crazy liberal nutcases, unhinged, need a rubber room, straitjacket people!"

Do you see anything like this going on out there or is it just me— regardless of the issue!

Chapter 10 Elites No Longer Elite—Too Bad!

Why did Edmund Burke know so much?

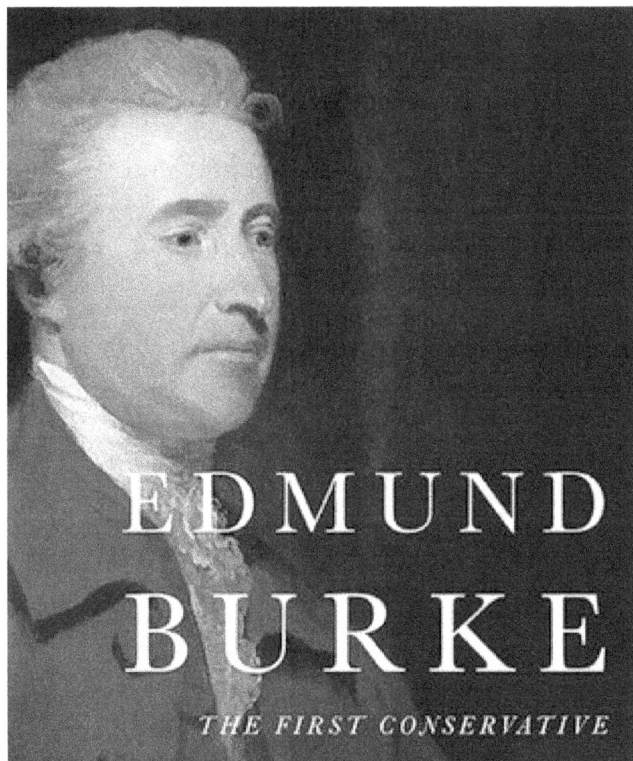

EDMUND BURKE

THE FIRST CONSERVATIVE

In 1774 the English Whig Party member and Political philosopher Edmund Burke offered that representatives should be elected to govern rather than the people directly. Burke did not think ordinary people could govern. I think he is right. But, only because as a group; we choose not to "pay attention!

He saw that such "elite" representatives should exercise their superior wisdom and judgment irrespective of the wishes of the electorate. That may be tough to take but consider what we get today. The electorate of his time in Burke's eyes would be easily characterized as "the low information voters," who are a huge part of "We the People." He saw their governance as being aided by an elitist private service--not a public service. How can people with no concern for government, govern? You tell me!

For Burke, it was not only OK to have an elite group that actually were virtuous, and who understood the laws; he would deem it very desirable. He believed that the public would always reject the "necessary hard decisions," and thus would be incapable of meaningful governance. Today we would call him naive but back then, there appears to have been a substantially higher level of integrity in the political class, thereby making his ideas more acceptable for the times.

Today, the progressive socialist Marxists pull at the heartstrings of the poor suggesting their days are numbered if an honest government is ever elected. How sick.

Many, including the framers of our Constitution were influenced by Burke but the elitists envisioned by Burke in his writings were not greedy politicians and corporate profiteers who also happened to be wealthy. For Burke, the elitists were in fact the elite of society, the cream of the crop by all standards. They were the best in character, education, and intelligence. They looked for nothing for themselves. They were the ultimate altruists. We can still find such men and women today if we stop listening to the disgusting press.

In their days, they were people you would like if you met them. They were not pretentious. They just happened to be better schooled and in many ways more intelligent and more capable of grappling through the tough decisions. The overall Edmund Burke philosophy is no longer acceptable to a vast number of people, though it is still promulgated by elitist editorialists, bureaucrats and some academicians. It is a great idea!

The problem with this notion is the tacit acceptance of an indefinable inequality and the fact that the good unquoted elite can very easily become members of the bad quoted elite, a group who are well characterized by taking substantially more than they give back. Today's plague of the gullible low information voter is the exact opposite of Burke's Law, yet there are so many in the gullible category, the progressive socialist propagandists suck them in one by one to their ultimate deaths.

As I have used it, you now see the new term that has been popularized by conservatives as "low information voters." This term was created to help define in few words those Americans who have no time to learn the facts, and who are gullible enough to believe everything the corrupt press and the party of progressive socialist Marxists chooses to propagandize to them. Yes, they can also be called dummies, and they often earn that name.

No Secrets!

The more eyes that look at the machinations of government, the safer and more prosperous we all will be. There are many arguments against open government at all levels, but history tells us that secrecy is a formula for corruption and long-term failure. Additionally, secrecy in government all too often provides for the perpetrators to avoid the responsibility and accountability that would be required if their actions were well known.

The fact is that corruption scandals are regular occurrences in governments across the world, and as you examine these failings, secrecy is always a required ingredient. If government is not always open, then what is it? It is closed of course—closed to the people and the free press.

If it is truly closed then how is it that in this closed scenario, the secret decision-making is always known by a privileged few who most certainly profit from the knowledge?

As open as our government is on paper, secret meetings are commonplace. Thus, we must be wary since these closed sessions occur with "our" representatives at all levels. When they are out of sight in secrecy, we can bet that they are representing somebody other than "We the People."

With a mostly educated populace as exists in the 21st century, it is in fact dangerous to merely trust our representatives with our government. We must also pay attention to their actions. The founders expected the people to not only pay attention, but to give our representatives instructions about how we expected affairs to be conducted. Most Americans today unfortunately are ill equipped to provide those instructions. We must change that.

We can be assured that unwatched representatives will not do the right thing. We must, as Ronald Reagan would say "trust but verify." It is all too easy for elected representatives and even their minions, and the bureaucrats, to assume that a shroud of wisdom comes down on them once they have arrived in their official chairs. But, of course it does not.

It is so much easier to serve the private rather than the public interest when dressed in the veil of secrecy, steering clear of accountability. Without a doubt, our most recent history furnishes abundant proof. Open the shades and bring in the light of day. Open the windows, please, and let the stink out of the room--for good. We get the government we deserve.

This Sums it up!

The Representative Democracy that our forefathers brought to this country is clearly not functioning properly in our times. Donald Trump is finding resistance from the swamp he vowed to destroy because they are self-serving and corrupt. Our elected representatives at all levels of government view the notion of representatives in a much more opportunistic way than intended by the Constitution and most other laws.

To solve this problem, we must admit that government is out of control and no longer is of the people, for the people, and by thy people. More importantly, we must have the guts to correct it, even if it means not getting something for ourselves from the largesse pile.

Yes, that means that even the nephew may be excluded from government largesse if we do the right thing. The time to fix it is now, perhaps before those really in charge become aware of their full power and we never have the opportunity again to regain control. The time is now. We get the government we deserve.

Chapter 11 What Happened to Representative Government?

What happened after the American Revolution?

- 1787 a group of leaders met in Philadelphia
- Constitution was written
- Model for new democracies around the world
- Great debate over strong vs. weak government
- Set up a representative government
- Federal government was formed

The partial list of issues of today

The list below makes the problem with Andrew Cuomo and the millennials look like small potatoes.

Something happened to representative government from the time of the Declaration of Independence and the Constitution to the present. Though our representative constitutional democracy (our Republic) has survived for about 240 years, it was not at its healthiest at the inception of the new president's term. right now. Here are just a few of the major problems that we are facing as a nation presented in alphabetic sequence:

- China preparing for a power grab
- Russia, Russia, Russia,

- Corporate power and greed
- Crime / Drugs
- Economic hard times just beginning to improve
- Education
- Election process corruption
- Energy and oil stagnation
- Excessive legal immigration
- Free trade hurts domestic producers
- Government Health industry power grab
- H-1B and D-1 Foreign National Visas
- Healthcare availability and affordability
- Homeland Security
- Illegal immigration
- -- 30 to 60 million illegal residents in shadows on welfare
- Influence of special Interests
- Institution of marriage
- Iran and North Korean as nuclear powers
- Israel second thinking American promises
- Jobs
- L-1A and L-1B Foreign National Visas
- Labor arbitrage / offshoring
- Lobbying
- Media in bed with Democratic Party
- Media fake news attack on President Trump
- Mexico dictating immigration policy
- Over taxation
- Political and corporate corruption
- Private property confiscation
- Respect for life
- Russia out of control; attacking its neighbors
- Russia Fake news
- Social Security / Medicare financial issues
- Syria mocking American red lines
- Threat of Socialism from the Government
- Unfinished wars in Iraq, Afghanistan (not really done)
- Unprecedented US weakness on the foreign front
- War on terrorism (whatever they call it now)

No book can attack all of these issues (listed in alphabetic order) and be substantive enough to be informative. This book does not even try. In this book, rather than thump the reader about all of these issues, we concentrate on the great elements of our founding as a country that would be included in any syllabus attempting to teach us about how to make America great again using our fundamental principles and beliefs.

Having been spawned by Cuomo and the millennials, we discuss elements of the founding and the structure of the government so that Americans can be reminded that this country was always great! It can be better, however! I hope we do OK

Throughout this book, besides the case v Cuomo and the millennials, we present notions that are included in our history and generally in our founding documents that can help you in understanding the lawful solutions to many issues outlined above and even more. But, nobody can handle them all in a single book, no matter what they say. I would answer in the affirmative if queried.

America is a great place with a great set of principles. My objective as I have noted many times between page 1 and this page, is to help all readers appreciate what gifts we have been given at our founding, and why they are important for your liberty and freedom. More importantly, I caution all Americans to not be chumps and do not believe in the people who represent us unless they have proven their worth and continue to prove their worth every day in office.

And, while we're at it, as a starter, there are a few things that we already know about that are intrinsically wrong. I bet nobody out there thinks it is OK that the government is spying on us when we walk, when we talk, and when we use the tools of the day such as the Internet, Facebook, Email, Twitter etc. Who likes the fact that 16,500 new IRS agents were hired by the prior president to assure that we are all buying Obamacare? Only an idiot would like any of that. An idiot needs a full education today just to become a dummy.

Nobody likes Big Brother; nonetheless Big Brother is growing because trusting Americans give him more and more power over our lives. That is why people like me and many others are writing in blogs, writing articles, and doing what we can to wake up the rest of our little brothers so that together we can save America before America is no more.

Nobody wants to wake up in an America a few years away when we can no longer vote in honest elections. Without honest elections, how will we ever remove the scoundrels who have corrupted our government? Unfortunately, many of the people who do not like what is happening today have yet to experience a voting machine. Folks, it is up to US to make this right again!

You have already been lightly introduced to the notion of a Constitutional Republic / Representative Democracy and you have already heard about the major checks and balances on government authority in the Constitution such as the separation of powers. I hope you have been paying attention.

This book discusses the bottom line reasons for why it is difficult to earn a living today and It presents a unique look at the disdain the founders had for large powerful entities such as unions and corporations and governments. Admittedly, it is getting better with Trump at the helm. If you think you have a lot of muscle and you need no help, try going against any of the big three in the power list above. That's why we elected Donald J. Trump.

Our congressional representatives, and presidential representatives (Yes, even the current and past president) are supposed to administer the will of the people. With our help, their jobs are to deal with all of the issues in the big list above as well as others that come up daily. The people are in charge!

In the last two elections before 2016, while in the midst of the presidential campaigns, through various forms of media, Americans were able to see the opinions and the to-do lists of all presidential aspirants. We saw what they thought about the issues and what they would do to "change" things for the better.

Each election time, the politicos come back home to put on a show with the intention of selling US on putting them back into office. They do not care whether we had gotten anything for our previously spent dimes. They hope we do not remember and typically we do not. And, the shame is that most often our dimes are lost. We have to stop that and pay more attention. Their motto is "Never give a sucker an even break and Never Smarten up a Chump." We cannot afford to be suckers or chumps for a government wanting to steal our freedom and liberty.

Hope and change are winners

Going back a way, change certainly was the theme in 2008's presidential primaries and it continued into the general election. Along the way, we even learned from the late John McCain and Mitt Romney that Washington was not only broke; it was broken and needed a quick, yet lasting repair.

Now, with Barack Obama running the Deep State, and President Trump dealing with Obama's leftover resistance, the country is on a fast track to success but from the Obama days, America is broke . There is a major concern that Obama's quick fix may have taken us right into Carl Marx's playbook, not from the founders. But, Americans did say no to a third term with Hillary. What do you think?

Promises, promises, promises. How can you tell when a politician is lying? The comic answer of course is, "When their lips are moving." That's because there is a big difference in the spoken words of politicians prior to the election and after being elected.

During the election process, promising politicians sell themselves and their ideas to the people using the level of promises necessary to get the vote. Nobody in the campaign team can say anything negative about the candidate or a proposed solution to an issue even if it is the truth.

If you can't get a promise from a politician pre-election, one thing is for sure. You will never get one after the election. Once elected, all bets are off and the truth and facts and real intentions of the politicians take over.

Unfortunately for the American people, when politicians as legislators, choose not to fulfill the essence of their promises, we cannot take them back to the store and get a new one. However, if we were to adopt the Recall Amendment to the Constitution, which I mention in this book, we would be able to take them back one more time to Washington, and then send them packing.

In addition to no recalls—at least yet, we cannot assess a penalty for lying to us about their real intentions. Initiative, Referendum, and Recall are direct democracy principles that are necessary today. They exist in 20 states but not at the federal level. So, we often wind up being stuck with politicians instead of being supported by our elected representatives. That is why it is important to know who to place on the ballot and who should get our votes long before election day. Pay attention!

Other Books by Brian W. Kelly: (amazon.com, and Kindle)

White People Are Bad! Bad! Bad! In 2018, too many people find race as a non-equalizer.
It's Time for The John Doe Party... Don't you think? By By Elephants.
Great Players in Florida Gators Football... Tim Tebow and a ton of other great players
Great Coaches in Florida Gators Football... The best coaches in Gator history.
The Constitution by Hamilton, Jefferson, Madison, et al. The Real Constitution
The Constitution Companion. Will help you learn and understand the Constitution
Great Coaches in Clemson Football The best Clemson Coaches right to Dabo Swinney
Great Players in Clemson Football The best Clemson players in history
Winning Back America. America's been stolen and can be won back completely
The Founding of America... Great book to pick up a lot of great facts
Defeating America's Career Politicians. The scoundrels need to go.
Midnight Mass by Jack Lammers... You remember what it was like Hreat story
The Bike by Jack Lammers... Great heartwarming Story by Jack
Wipe Out All Student Loan Debt--Now! Watch the economy go boom!
No Free Lunch Pay Back Welfare! Why not pay it back?
Deport All Millennials Now!!! Why they deserve to be deported and/or saved
DELETE the EPA, Please! The worst decisions to hurt America
Taxation Without Representation 4th Edition Should we throw the TEA overboard again?
Four Great Political Essays by Thomas Dawson
Top Ten Political Books for 2018... Cliffnotes Version of 10 Political Books
Top Six Patriotic Books for 2018... Cliffnotes version of 6 Patriotic Boosk
Why Trump Got Elected!.. It's great to hear about a great milestone in America!
The Day the Free Press Died. Corrupt Press Lives on!
Solved (Immigration) The best solutions for 2018
Solved II (Obamacare, Social Security, Student Debt) Check it out; They're solved.
Great Moments in Pittsburgh Steelers Football... Six Super Bowls and more.
Great Players in Pittsburgh Steelers Football ,,,Chuck Noll, Bill Cowher, Mike Tomin, etc.
Great Coaches in New England Patriots Football,,, Bill Belichick the one and only plus others
Great Players in New England Patriots Football... Tom Brady, Drew Bledsoe et al.
Great Coaches in Philadelphia Eagles Football..Andy Reid, Doug Pederson & Lots more
Great Players in Philadelphia Eagles Football Great players such as Sonny Jurgenson
Great Coaches in Syracuse Football All the greats including Ben Schwartzwalder
Great Players in Syracuse Football. Highlights best players such as Jim Brown & Donovan McNabb
Millennials are People Too !!! Give US millennials help to live American Dream
Brian Kelly for the United States Senate from PA: Fresh Face for US Senate
The Candidate's Bible. Don't pray for your campaign without this bible
Rush Limbaugh's Platform for Americans... Rush will love it
Sean Hannity's Platform for Americans... Sean will love it
Donald Trump's New Platform for Americans. Make Trump unbeatable in 2020
Tariffs Are Good for America! One of the best tools a president can have
Great Coaches in Pittsburgh Steelers Football Sixteen of the best coaches ever to coach in pro football.
Great Moments in New England Patriots Football Great football moments from Boston to New England
Great Moments in Philadelphia Eagles Football. The best from the Eagles from the beginning of football.
Great Moments in Syracuse Football The great moments, coaches & players in Syracuse Football
Boost Social Security Now! Hey Buddy Can You Spare a Dime?
The Birth of American Football. From the first college game in 1869 to the last Super Bowl
Obamacare: A One-Line Repeal Congress must get this done.
A Wilkes-Barre Christmas Story A wonderful town makes Christmas all the better
A Boy, A Bike, A Train, and a Christmas Miracle A Christmas story that will melt your heart
Pay-to-Go   America-First Immigration Fix
Legalizing Illegal Aliens Via Resident Visas Americans-first plan saves $Trillions. Learn how!
60 Million Illegal Aliens in America!!! A simple, America-first solution.
The Bill of Rights By Founder James Madison Refresh your knowledge of the specific rights for all
Great Players in Army Football Great Army Football played by great players..
Great Coaches in Army Football Army's coaches are all great.
Great Moments in Army Football Army Football at its best.
Great Moments in Florida Gators Football Gators Football from the start. This is the book.
Great Moments in Clemson Football CU Football at its best. This is the book.
Great Moments in Florida Gators Football Gators Football from the start. This is the book.
The Constitution Companion. A Guide to Reading and Comprehending the Constitution
The Constitution by Hamilton, Jefferson, & Madison – Big type and in English

PATERNO: The Dark Days After Win # 409. Sky began to fall within days of win # 409.
JoePa 409 Victories: Say No More! Winningest Division I-A football coach ever
American College Football: The Beginning From before day one football was played.
Great Coaches in Alabama Football Challenging the coaches of every other program!
Great Coaches in Penn State Football the Best Coaches in PSU's football program
Great Players in Penn State Football The best players in PSU's football program
Great Players in Notre Dame Football The best players in ND's football program
Great Coaches in Notre Dame Football The best coaches in any football program
Great Players in Alabama Football from Quarterbacks to offensive Linemen Greats!
Great Moments in Alabama Football AU Football from the start. This is the book.
Great Moments in Penn State Football PSU Football, start--games, coaches, players,
Great Moments in Notre Dame Football ND Football, start, games, coaches, players
Cross Country with the Parents A great trip from East Coast to West with the kids
Seniors, Social Security & the Minimum Wage. Things seniors need to know.
How to Write Your First Book and Publish It with CreateSpace
The US Immigration Fix--It's all in here. Finally, an answer.
I had a Dream IBM Could be #1 Again The title is self-explanatory
WineDiets.Com Presents The Wine Diet Learn how to lose weight while having fun.
Wilkes-Barre, PA; Return to Glory Wilkes-Barre City's return to glory
Geoffrey Parsons' Epoch... The Land of Fair Play Better than the original.
The Bill of Rights 4 Dummmies! This is the best book to learn about your rights.
Sol Bloom's Epoch ...Story of the Constitution The best book to learn the Constitution
America 4 Dummmies! All Americans should read to learn about this great country.
The Electoral College 4 Dummmies! How does it really work?
The All-Everything Machine Story about IBM's finest computer server.
ThankYou IBM! This book explains how IBM was beaten in the computer marketplace by neophytes

Brian has written 173 books in total. Other books can be found at amazon.com/author/brianwkelly

www.ingramcontent.com/pod-product-compliance
Lightning Source LLC
Chambersburg PA
CBHW050530280326
41933CB00011B/1529